P9-BIV-267

Truth in the Eight Towers

Robert Leslie Palmer

CROSSBOOKS
PUBLISHING

CrossBooks™
A Division of LifeWay
1663 Liberty Drive
Bloomington, IN 47403
www.crossbooks.com
Phone: 1-866-879-0502

Scriptures taken from the Holy Bible, New International Version®, NIV®.
Copyright © 1973, 1978, 1984 by Biblica, Inc.™
Used by permission of Zondervan. All rights reserved worldwide.

Author photograph courtesy of Carri Bass Photography (www.carribass.com)

©2011 Robert Leslie Palmer. All rights reserved.

No part of this book may be reproduced, stored in a retrieval system, or
transmitted by any means without the written permission of the author.

First published by CrossBooks 05/05/2011

ISBN: 978-1-6150-7843-1 (sc)
ISBN: 978-1-6150-7844-8 (dj)

Library of Congress Control Number: 2011927992

Printed in the United States of America

This book is printed on acid-free paper.

Because of the dynamic nature of the Internet, any web addresses or links contained in
this book may have changed since publication and may no longer be valid. The views
expressed in this work are solely those of the author and do not necessarily reflect the
views of the publisher, and the publisher hereby disclaims any responsibility for them.

Dedication

This book is dedicated to my wife, **Huisuk Kim Palmer**, and my son, **Aaron Rowe Palmer**, whose love and encouragement made this book possible.

Contents

Dedication v
Acknowledgments ix

Overview 1
First Beatitude 5
Second Beatitude 21
Third Beatitude 39
Fourth Beatitude 53
Fifth Beatitude 71
Sixth Beatitude 85
Seventh Beatitude 99
Eighth Beatitude 115
The Kingdom of Heaven 131
Archie's Journey 135

Glossary 145
About the Book 157
About the Author 159

Acknowledgments

This book would not be possible had it not been for the loving support of my wife, **Huisuk Kim Palmer**, and son, **Aaron Rowe Palmer**, who not only encouraged me to write this book but supported my decision to take a sabbatical from the practice of law in order to do so. In addition, they both offered invaluable advice about the manuscript.

I am also indebted to several other people, mostly friends and family, who agreed to read my manuscript and make comments. They include my sisters, **Coralie Maples, Claire Ferguson**, and **Charlotte Podsednik**, my brother **Bill Palmer**, my sister-in-law, **Rennie Palmer**, and my niece, **Jasmine Lee**. My friends who reviewed the manuscript include **Carri Bass, David Bass, Anthony Cooper, Amelia deBuys, Ben Hogan, Bill Lewis, Susan McPherson, Clint Neumann, Erica Neumann, Ken Riddle, Siham Shunnarah, Barry Stalnaker**, and **Randy Tribble**. Although I could not incorporate all of the comments they made, I used the best suggestions to improve the book.

I am indebted to **Steve Drake** of **LifeWay**, who graciously reviewed my manuscript and checked the accuracy of the Greek and Hebrew, and **Phill Burgess** of **CrossBooks**, who also reviewed my manuscript and assisted me in many other ways. There are many others at **CrossBooks** who offered invaluable assistance, many whose names I do not know. I want to thank the very talented artist, **Mark Anthony Pino**, for his excellent artwork as well as for his patience in making the numerous changes I requested. I also thank **Kelly Barrow**, whose cover design is an exceptional expression of what I wanted to convey on the cover. Thanks also to **Sam Fitzgerald** for his invaluable assistance in the production of the book. I appreciate the hard work that **Joel Pierson** and his team put in to edit the novel. Finally, I would also like to thank **Rebecca Roberts, Matt Campbell, Brian Martindale**, and **Stefanie Holzbacher** for their assistance.

Overview

Ⅎn the last chapter of *Archibald Zwick and the Eight Towers,* Archie awakens to find himself in his bed at the vacation home his family is renting. He discovers that although he is still wearing the sacred necklace of K´truum-Shra, the inscriptions have changed. Before he awoke, the eight medallions each displayed one of the inscriptions Archie found on the eight towers, but in the last chapter, they display the Beatitudes. This is because the entire story is an allegory for the Christian journey through the Beatitudes. Because it is not possible to fully appreciate that allegory without first discussing the Beatitudes, my discussion of the allegory will be preceded by a thorough discussion of the Beatitudes.

What drew me to the Beatitudes is the fact that they begin the Sermon on the Mount. Having engaged in public speaking in my career, I was aware of the adage that a speaker should "tell them what you are going to tell them, then tell them, then tell them what you told them." This suggested to me that the Beatitudes constitute an introductory synopsis of the Sermon on the Mount—that distilled within these eight verses is the essence of that sermon.

Other than reading and studying the Bible since becoming a Christian, I have no theological training. But as an attorney, I have been trained in analytical thinking, and applying such thinking to Scripture is not unlike the analysis in which lawyers engage every day to determine what a particular statute, case, or constitutional provision means.

The structure of the Beatitudes says a great deal about them. First, each of the eight Beatitudes begins with the same word, "blessed." In addition, all eight of the Beatitudes make an "if-then" statement, referring first to a particular attribute and then to a promised blessing linked to that attribute. But the attributes to which the first seven beatitudes refer are all *internal* attributes, while the attribute described in the eighth and final beatitude is an *external* attribute. What I mean is that the attributes to which the first seven beatitudes refer describe the attitudes and behavior of the person being blessed, while the attribute described in the eighth beatitude describes behavior directed by others toward that person.

Finally, the Beatitudes begin and end with the same promise—the kingdom of heaven. It therefore occurred to me that perhaps this was a poetic device intended to show that the Beatitudes are really about one thing: the way to the kingdom of heaven. That conclusion is supported by the fact that the promise of the kingdom in the last beatitude is linked to an external attribute, for that itself suggests a series of steps involving individual attitudes and behavior but culminating in the world's reaction to those attitudes and behavior. Thus, the very structure of the Beatitudes suggests that they describe how to find the kingdom of heaven—in short, how to become a Christian and mature in the faith.

To really understand any Scripture, it is sometimes necessary to study that Scripture in the context of the original language in which it was written and the culture to which it was addressed. Because I am not a Greek or Hebrew scholar, I turned to two reference works written in part to help those not literate in biblical Greek or Hebrew, *The Strongest Strong's Exhaustive Concordance of the Bible*[1] and the *New International Dictionary of New Testament Theology*.[2] Every reference herein to the meaning of particular Greek or Hebrew words is based on those valuable references.

The Greek word in each of the Beatitudes that is translated as "blessed" is μακαριος ("makarios"),[3] which literally means "fortunate" or "happy."[4] It originally meant to be "free from daily cares or worries,"[5] and the happiness to which "makarios" refers is not merely a mood dependent upon external circumstance but an internal state of happiness. That internal state of happiness can exist only when one places his trust in God rather than

---

1   James Strong, LLD, STD, *The Strongest Strong's Exhaustive Concordance of the Bible.* Fully revised and corrected by John R. Kohlenberger III and James A. Swanson. Grand Rapids, MI: Zondervan, 2001. Hereinafter referred to as *"Strong's."* Some of the references to *"Strong's"* are to the electronic version included with the Bible study software, QuickVerse 3.0h, hereinafter referred to as *Strong's-QuickVerse.*

2   Verlyn D. Verbrugge, *New International Dictionary of New Testament Theology.* Grand Rapids, MI: Zondervan, 2000. Hereinafter referred to as *"Theology."* This work uses the Goodrick-Kohlenberger ("GK") categorization of Greek words.

3   *Strong's,* G3107; *Theology,* GK3421.

4   *Strong's,* G3107.

5   *Theology,* GK3421.

in his own "righteousness."[6] This, too, suggested to me that the Beatitudes are not only an introduction to the Sermon on the Mount but a synopsis of God's plan of salvation.

---

6   See, for example, Psalm 2:11–12; Psalm 32:1–2; Psalm 34:8; Psalm 40:4; Psalm 84:12; Psalm 89:15; Psalm 112:1; Psalm 119:2; and Psalm 128:4.

We are poor in spirit when we know that we must rely on God for righteousness just as the beggar knows he must rely on others for money.

First Beatitude

"Blessed are the poor in spirit, for theirs is the kingdom of heaven."

—Matthew 5:3

Jesus begins his Sermon on the Mount with a phrase—"poor in spirit"—that appears nowhere else in the Bible. The word translated as "poor" is πτωχος ("ptōchos"),[7] which literally means "beggar."[8] It refers to an individual so destitute that he must rely on other people for the necessities of life. What is important about the word is not its description of the person's financial state but rather his attitude about that condition. The root word πτωσσω ("ptōsso")[9] literally means to "crouch"[10] or cower down in fear, and it is also related to two other Greek words,[11] πτοεω ("ptoeō"),[12] meaning "to be terrified,"[13] and πιπτω ("piptō"),[14] meaning to "fall" or "bow down."[15] Furthermore, in the culture in which Jesus preached, poverty was often associated with seeking God, for the poor had no one else on whom they could rely.[16]

---

7   *Strong's*, G4434; *Theology*, GK4777.
8   *Strong's*, G4434.
9   The root word does not appear in the Bible and therefore is not numbered in *Strong's* and is apparently not mentioned in *Theology*. Also, it is mentioned only in *Strong's-QuickVerse*.
10   *Strong's-QuickVerse*.
11   *Strong's-QuickVerse*.
12   *Strong's*, G4422.
13   Ibid.
14   *Strong's*, G4098; *Theology*, GK4406.
15   Ibid.
16   The poor were often viewed as innocent victims of injustice (e.g., Ps. 37:14; Prov. 13:23; Isa. 3:14; 10:1–2) whose only refuge was the Lord (Ps. 14:6; 40:17; 112:9; 140:12; Isa. 11:3–4). However, sometimes the poor were blamed for their own condition (e.g., Prov. 10:4).

Thus, the picture painted by the Greek word "ptōchos" is far different than that painted by the English word "poor," which merely suggests a person lacking financial means. Instead, the Greek word paints the picture of a beggar who is so ashamed of his condition that he is terrified of the people from whom he must seek charity, and so he falls down before them. A beggar would do this only if he sincerely believed not only that he was entirely unworthy of the gift he seeks but even of mere contact with the giver.

But Jesus did not simply refer to beggars as he began his sermon but beggars *in spirit*. The Greek word that has been translated as "spirit" is πνευμα ("pneuma"),[17] which literally means "wind," "breath," "blast," or "breeze,"[18] but also refers to the spirit. Under Stoic influence, the word had come to refer to an actual material substance that filled the human body and made a person able to prophesy.[19] But as used by Jesus in the first beatitude, "pneuma" refers to the human spirit—that part of a person most open and receptive to God.[20]

A beggar has accepted the fact that he is not self-sufficient and that he must therefore seek financial grace from another. One who is a "beggar in spirit," then, is one who recognizes that he is not righteous and that he must seek spiritual grace from another—that is, from God. In short, one who is "poor in spirit" knows that he is a sinner and that he is in need of God's grace. And although we may generally "acknowledge" that we are sinners, most of us still believe deep down that we are "good people" and that our sins are minor. That is not the kind of thinking that Jesus is talking about. Isaiah, a prophet whose writings Jesus often quoted, tells us:

> All of us have become like one who is unclean, and all our
> righteous acts are like filthy rags; we all shrivel up like a leaf,
> and like the wind our sins sweep us away (Isa. 64:6).[21]

The Hebrew word translated as "rag" is בֶּגֶד ("beged"),[22] which literally means a "covering,"[23] meaning a garment.[24] It is significant that the metaphor of a garment is often used in the Bible to refer to righteousness received

---

17 *Strong's*, G4151; *Theology*, GK4460.
18 Ibid.
19 *Theology*, GK4460.
20 Ibid. See also Luke 1:47, Romans 1:9, 1 Corinthians 2, and 1 Peter 3:4.
21 See also Job 15:14–16.
22 *Strong's*, H899.
23 *Strong's-QuickVerse*.
24 Ibid.

from God, for that righteousness covers our own lack of righteousness. For example, Job declared, "I put on righteousness as my clothing; justice was my robe and my turban."[25] Even in one of the parables that Jesus used to describe the kingdom of heaven, the parable of the wedding banquet,[26] the man who chooses not to wear the wedding clothes provided for him is thrown out. And in Revelation we are told that those saved by God will receive "white robes" that cover their sin.[27]

But Isaiah is not talking about righteousness received from God. The Hebrew word translated as "filthy" is עִד ("iddâ," "éd," or "ayd"),[28] which literally referred to an appointed time. It was commonly intended to refer to a woman's menstrual flow,[29] which was ritually unclean under Old Testament law.[30] This brings us back to the Hebrew word "beged," which can mean not only "garment" but also "treachery"[31]—in other words, deceit. Thus, when Isaiah tells us that "all our righteous acts are like filthy rags," his choice of words even suggests that *we deceive ourselves if we think that we have any righteousness apart from God.*[32] And the strength of Isaiah's declaration can be found in the fact that he did not merely tell us that our *sins* are filthy, or even that *we* are filthy, but that our *"righteous acts"* are filthy! He is telling us that even what we see as "righteous" in ourselves is actually sinful, and that if we rely on our own righteousness, we deceive ourselves, for our righteousness is only an illusion.

Even in Psalms we encounter the question, "Who can discern his errors?"[33] This is a question that we must daily ask ourselves if we want to avoid deceiving ourselves about our own righteousness. Indeed, we must force ourselves to see our own tendency to make ourselves "righteous" by classifying and categorizing sins. We tell ourselves that our own sins are lesser sins and then conclude that we are therefore "basically good" people. But consider the following example.

Three people who all live in the same residential neighborhood drive home from work, tired from the day's labors. When they reach their neighborhood, all three of them drive thirty-five miles per hour even

---

25 Job 29:14.
26 Matthew 22:11–14.
27 Revelation 6:11.
28 *Strong's*, H5708.
29 Ibid.
30 See Leviticus 15:19–30.
31 *Strong's*, H5708.
32 "If we claim to be without sin, we deceive ourselves and the truth is not in us" (1 John 1:8).
33 Psalm 19:12.

though the posted speed limit is twenty miles per hour. The first arrives home without incident. The second is stopped by a police officer and given a speeding ticket. But the third accidentally strikes and kills a four-year-old child who darts in front of his vehicle.

All three neighbors committed the identical offense by breaking a law that was intended to protect children like the one killed by the third driver. But the consequences of their identical offenses varied greatly. It is unlikely that anyone other than the first driver would ever know that he committed that offense, and if he was even aware that he was breaking the law, even he was likely to soon forget. The second driver might mention the offense and the ticket to his wife and friends but will also escape any serious judgment. But the unfortunate third driver faces not only potential prison time for manslaughter but also a civil lawsuit from the child's parents. And when we hear of the third driver's arrest, conviction, or bankruptcy, we tend to judge the severity of his offense by the *consequences* that he suffered. Otherwise we condemn ourselves, for most of us are probably guilty of the very same offense.[34] If we don't make the third driver's offense more serious in our own minds, then we are troubled by our own conduct, and we do not like that at all. Put another way, if we see our own conduct as identical to that of the third driver, as we should, then we will never again break the residential speed limit.

It is interesting that Christians frequently quote Romans 3:23, declaring that "all have sinned and fall short of the glory of God," but do so without realizing that the sentence they are quoting neither begins nor ends in that verse. Indeed, many would be surprised to find that the sentence begins in verse 22 with the words, "There is no difference."

Although Paul was responding to those who sought to make distinctions between Jewish and Gentile believers,[35] he was explaining that true righteousness comes from God through faith in Christ. Indeed, it is clear that the very reason Paul penned these lines is that the Jewish believers to whom Paul was addressing his comment were trying to exalt themselves because of their "adherence" to the Old Testament law. In short, they were apparently relying on their own "righteous acts."[36] They just could not accept the fact that sin is sin, without grade or distinction. During his ministry, Jesus made this very point:[37]

---

34   See Romans 2:1.
35   See Romans 3:9–20 and Romans 10:11–13.
36   See Matthew 23:23–28.
37   See also Matthew 5:21–32.

Now there were some present at that time who told Jesus about the Galileans whose blood Pilate had mixed with their sacrifices. Jesus answered, "Do you think that these Galileans were worse sinners than all the other Galileans because they suffered this way? I tell you, no! But unless you repent, you too will all perish. Or those eighteen who died when the tower in Siloam fell on them—do you think they were more guilty than all the others living in Jerusalem? I tell you, no! But unless you repent, you too will all perish" (Luke 13:1–5).

And today though the divisions may not be as clear as those between Jewish and Gentile believers that Paul addressed in the early church, we nevertheless continue to differentiate between "acceptable" and "unacceptable" sins. That is why we welcome practicing gluttons into our congregations with open hearts, but look with suspicion upon other sinners whose sins we believe are worse. We still have difficulty accepting the fact that there are no degrees of sin, and that one is either a sinner or not, just as one is either pregnant or not, or dead or not. And, of course, only Jesus was without sin, so even this is a false dichotomy when we apply it to ourselves.

Unfortunately, this is a difficult concept even for professing Christians, for our pride gets in the way. When his disciples were arguing over which of them would be greater in the kingdom of heaven, Jesus pointed out their folly by calling a child to his side and then saying to his disciples:

"… unless you change and become like little children, you will never enter the kingdom of heaven. Therefore, whoever humbles himself like this child is the greatest in the kingdom of heaven" (Matt. 18:3–4).

It is interesting that both the first beatitude and this declaration concern entry into the kingdom of heaven. So important was this point that Jesus repeatedly declared that self-righteousness is not righteousness at all:

To some who were confident of their own righteousness and looked down on everybody else, Jesus told this parable: "Two men went up to the temple to pray, one a Pharisee and the other a tax collector. The Pharisee stood up and prayed about himself: 'God, I thank you that I am not like other men—robbers, evildoers, adulterers—or even like this tax collector. I fast twice a week and give a tenth of all I get.' But the tax collector stood at a distance. He would not even look up to heaven, but beat his breast and said, 'God, have mercy on me, a sinner.' I tell you that this man, rather than the other, went home justified before God. For everyone who exalts himself will be humbled, and he who humbles himself will be exalted." (Luke 18:9–14).

It is as true today as it was when Jesus spoke, and indeed, in the time of the Old Testament, that the "sacrifices of God are a broken spirit."[38] Humility is the first step in becoming a Christian, and continued humility is just as important in maturing in the faith.

---

38   Psalm 51:17.

Questions for Further Study of the First Beatitude

List your "righteous" acts, those acts in which you have taken pride. Why are you proud of these acts? What was your motivation for performing these "righteous" acts? What actions did you take that reveal your true motives?

_____

_____

_____

_____

_____

_____

_____

_____

_____

_____

_____

_____

_____

_____

_____

_____

_____

_____

_____

_____

_____

_____

_____

_____

_____

_____

_____

_____

Identify three people in the Bible who were poor in spirit. What actions or attitudes make it clear that they were poor in spirit? What led them to become poor in spirit? How are their actions and attitudes different from your own? How are they the same?

Identify three people in the Bible who were self-righteous. What actions or attitudes make it clear that they were self-righteous? How are their actions and attitudes different from your own? How are they the same?

_____

_____

_____

_____

_____

_____

_____

_____

_____

_____

_____

_____

_____

_____

_____

_____

_____

_____

_____

_____

_____

_____

_____

_____

Does being poor in spirit require you to despise yourself? Is self-loathing the same as humility? If you have no real righteousness, do you have any value or worth? If so, then what gives you that worth? If not, then why did God create you, and why would God die for you on the cross?

_____

_____

_____

_____

_____

_____

_____

_____

_____

_____

_____

_____

_____

_____

_____

_____

_____

_____

_____

_____

_____

_____

_____

_____

_____

_____

_____

_____

Blessed are the Poor in Spirit
by Robert Leslie Palmer

How can I deny my remarkable worth,
Crafted by architect of heaven and earth?

Unwilling to slander Your Holy Name,
How can I explain my awful shame?

Made lovingly by One so flawless and holy,
Sin has rendered me but filthy and lowly.

Impossible dreams I can never achieve,
Only failed virtue I always must grieve.

Lord, You made me, so how can I be,
Eternally happy, from sin set free?

Is my great value not in self alone?
No! It is in service to Your grand throne!

That apart from You, I am mere dust,
Destined to vanish through windy gust!

You, Creator, knew me before birth,
And union with You fulfills my worth.

We mourn in the sense of the second Beatitude
when our grief over our sins leads us to repent.

Second Beatitude

"Blessed are those who mourn, for they will be comforted."

—Matthew 5:4

Jesus continues his introduction to the Sermon on the Mount by quoting from the prophet Isaiah,[39] giving a second blessing for what may at first appear to be conduct unrelated to the humility blessed in the first beatitude. Simply reading the second beatitude in English creates the impression of a loving God holding us and comforting us in times of sorrow and trouble, but no more than that.

If the Beatitudes are independent of each other—and therefore devoid of context—then the word "mourn" could have a number of different meanings. But if the Beatitudes are related and show a progression from sin and death to repentance and salvation and then to spiritual growth, to mourn in this context logically means to regret one's sinful nature and spiritual "death" and to possess a heart prepared for repentance. This conclusion is supported by the language of the blessing itself.

The Greek word translated as "mourn" is πενθεω ("pentheō"),[40] which literally means to "grieve," "mourn," or "wail."[41] The word is the strongest Greek word for "mourn" and is often used to refer to those who mourn the dead.[42] In the Middle East, such mourning is often accompanied by wailing. Significantly, Paul even used the term to refer to his grief over those who die without repenting their sins.[43]

---

39   Isaiah 61:2.
40   *Strong's*, G3996; *Theology*, GK4291.
41   Ibid.
42   *Theology*, GK4291.
43   Second Corinthians 12:21.

Thus, the picture painted by Jesus in the second beatitude is not just that of God comforting us in our times of sorrow but rather our interaction with God when, having recognized our own lack of righteousness, we mourn or grieve our own spiritual deaths. But God does not merely comfort us when we mourn our own sin—He calls us to repentance. This is where reference to the original Greek is most useful in the Beatitudes, for the Greek word translated as "comfort" is παρακαλεω ("parakaleō"),[44] which literally means "to call near."[45] It therefore means not only "comfort," but also "exhort," "invite," or "appeal."[46] One of its root words is καλεω[47] ("kaleō"), which can be translated either as "call" or "invite,"[48] but these are not really unrelated concepts. Even in English we refer to a "calling," meaning work that God bids us to do.

In the second beatitude, then, Jesus is not merely saying that God will comfort us when we mourn our own sin but that God will then invite us to repent. Support for this conclusion comes from the use of the word "kaleō" throughout the New Testament, but most notably in the parable of the wedding banquet. Jesus uses the word "kaleō" five times in that parable and then concludes it by declaring about the man who refused to wear the wedding clothes provided by the king hosting the banquet, "For many are invited, but few are chosen."[49]

Thus, even in other places in the New Testament, the invitation to repentance that is the subject of the second beatitude is closely linked to the awareness of our own sinful natures that is the subject of the first beatitude. That is why Jesus rebuked the Pharisees and teachers of the law, saying, "I have not come to call the righteous, but sinners to repentance."[50] He clearly was not saying that the Pharisees were righteous, but rather that they failed to recognize that they were not. But more important, he was declaring that there would be no invitation to repentance until they recognized that all of their righteous acts were nothing more than the "filthy rags" to which Isaiah refers.

God does not call us to be humble for a brief moment, just long enough to repent our sins and accept salvation. Instead, we are called to be humble throughout the remainder of our lives. Our tendency toward self-

---

44   *Strong's*, G3870; *Theology*, GK4151.
45   *Strong's-QuickVerse.*
46   *Strong's*, G3870; *Theology*, GK4151.
47   *Strong's*, G2564; *Theology*, GK4291.
48   Ibid.
49   Matthew 22:14.
50   Luke 5:32.

righteousness is so ingrained that even as we go to church and "worship" God, we slowly forget just how we got there in the first place, and we begin to build our own "righteousness" portfolios, which we proudly display each Sunday. But our true nature is revealed in the way we regard other sinners who have not yet found their way back to God. Jesus spoke of this attitude in at least two parables, the parable of the prodigal son[51] and the parable of the workers in the field.[52] In each of these parables there is a lesson about the resentment toward "lesser" believers. The prodigal son's brother was clearly self-righteous, as were the first workers hired to work the field. And in each parable, Jesus rebuked that attitude. If we have truly mourned our own sins and our spiritual deaths so that we have repented, then we will bear this in mind for the rest of our lives, and it will be evident in the way we interact not only with new believers, but even with unbelievers. As Paul put it, "Godly sorrow brings repentance that leads to salvation and leaves no regret, but worldly sorrow brings death."[53]

---

51   Luke 15:11–32.
52   Matthew 20:1–16.
53   Second Corinthians 7:10.

Questions for Further Study of the Second Beatitude

List as many of your sins as you can recall, beginning with the ones you regard as the worst. Be sure to list both sins of commission (sinful actions you have taken) and sins of omission (actions you have sinfully failed to take). Be sure to also include sinful thoughts.

_____

_____

_____

_____

_____

_____

_____

_____

_____

_____

_____

_____

_____

_____

_____

_____

_____

_____

_____

_____

_____

_____

_____

_____

_____

Was there enough room above to list all of your sins? How much paper would be required to do so? Are you even able to recall all of your sins? Do you believe that you are even aware of all your sins? How does this make you feel about yourself?

_____

_____

_____

_____

_____

_____

_____

_____

_____

_____

_____

_____

_____

_____

_____

_____

_____

_____

_____

_____

_____

_____

_____

_____

_____

_____

_____

How can you change and repent your sins? Is it possible to turn from your sins if you refuse to think about them? Is it possible to repent a sin of which you are not aware? Why do you think God has commanded you to confess your sins? Does confession benefit God or you? Is it possible to turn from your sins without God's help?

Are there any sins that you try to hide from others? Are there any sins that you try to hide from yourself? Are there any sins that you try to hide from God? Are your attempts to hide your sin from others, from yourself, and from God successful? If not, why not?

_____

_____

_____

_____

_____

_____

_____

_____

_____

_____

_____

_____

_____

_____

_____

_____

_____

_____

_____

_____

_____

_____

_____

_____

_____

_____

_____

_____

_____

_____

_____

How does your *knowledge* of your sin – as opposed to the sin itself – affect your relationship with God? How does it affect your relationship with other sinners? How does knowledge of your sin make you feel about the sins of others, particularly those who have sinned against you?

_____

_____

_____

_____

_____

_____

_____

_____

_____

_____

_____

_____

_____

_____

_____

_____

_____

_____

_____

_____

_____

_____

_____

_____

_____

_____

_____

_____

_____

_____

_____

Does knowledge of your sinfulness give birth to any desire? If so, what is that desire, and what is the source of that desire?

_____

_____

_____

_____

_____

_____

_____

_____

_____

_____

_____

_____

_____

_____

_____

_____

_____

_____

_____

_____

_____

_____

_____

_____

_____

_____

Blessed are Those Who Mourn

by Robert Leslie Palmer

Moans will never erase my shameful guilt,
Nor eradicate the dire fate I've built.

Outcast from Hope, stranger to Paradise,
How can I, a pauper, pay the price?

Unhappy soul, with ought but filthy rags adorned,
Unhappy fate, unending Death now gravely mourned!

Righteousness I once boasted that I wore,
Proved false, no better than a filthy whore!

Now I know salvation I can never earn,
To God alone, humbled, I must turn.

Into His eyes I now meekly look,
Expecting judgment, shocked by what He took!

Nailed to the cross, He bore my sins,
So if to Him I turn, my soul He wins!

God in His mercy my future has built,
For He alone erases my shameful guilt.

We are meek when we put others first, as Jesus
demonstrated by washing the disciples' feet.

Third Beatitude

"Blessed are the meek, for they will inherit the earth."
—Matthew 5:5

While the first two beatitudes concern the steps that lead us to God's free offer of salvation, the third beatitude concerns our acceptance of that offer and the attitude that accompanies and follows that acceptance—meekness. This is made clear by the Scripture that Jesus quotes in the third beatitude, for just as Jesus quoted the prophet Isaiah in the second beatitude, He quotes Psalms in the third: "But the meek will inherit the land and enjoy great peace."[54] What makes it clear that the "meek" include only those who accept the free gift of salvation by trusting in the Lord is the variation of the declaration made just two verses earlier in the Psalm: "For evil men will be cut off, but those who hope in the Lord will inherit the land."[55]

But just what is the attitude with which we accept the offer of salvation and trust in the Lord? The Greek word translated as "meek" is πραυς ("praus"),[56] which literally means "gentle" or "humble."[57] Significantly, it is a word that is used to refer to an animal that has been "broken" so that it will submit to its master.[58] Its use in another verse illustrates just what it means to be "meek." In the same passage that directs wives to submit

---

54 Psalm 37:11.
55 Psalm 37:9. The prophet Zephaniah similarly associates meekness with trusting in the Lord (Zeph. 2:3; 3:11–12).
56 *Strong's*, G4239; *Theology*, GK4558.
57 Ibid. Indeed, it is often translated as "gentle." See, for example, Matthew 21:5.
58 *Theology*, GK4558.

to their husbands, they are told that their beauty comes from this meek, or gentle, spirit.[59]

In the New Testament, the church is frequently referred to as the bride of Christ.[60] It therefore follows that the meekness to which the third beatitude refers includes submission to Christ, the Bridegroom. And Jesus Himself told us that He is the example of meekness.[61]

Just as pride is the opposite of humility, self-seeking is the opposite of meekness. We have been presented a clear choice—either serve ourselves, seeking our own interests, or serve God, seeking His will. It is impossible to do both, as Jesus warned us that "no one can serve two masters."[62]

Meekness will always be evident in one who has truly accepted God's free gift of salvation and truly trusted in God. Indeed, without meekness, it is impossible to obey the Bridegroom, for He has commanded us to love both God and our fellow human beings, and He has told us that these are the greatest commandments.[63] As long as our focus is inward, on ourselves, we cannot direct it outward, toward our neighbors. Whether characterized as meekness, gentleness, or self-control, meekness is always listed among Christian virtues,[64] and it is deemed to be a fruit of the Spirit.[65] Even when restoring fellow Christians who have gone astray, we are commanded to be meek.[66]

It is important to note that meekness is not the same as weakness. In fact, it takes great strength to be meek, and that is one reason it is impossible to be meek without trusting in the Lord. We can only truly become meek when we are looking beyond the here and now and relying on God's strength. Otherwise we could not surrender to God's will, or turn the other cheek[67] when wronged by a neighbor. But once meekness becomes a part of us, the effect is tremendous. For one thing, God is then free to use us as He sees fit, for we will actually seek His will and listen for that still, small voice that tells us His will. And when surrendered to God's will, we can accomplish things that we never would have dreamed possible. But if that is not enough, when we are meek, our neighbors—even those

---

59   First Peter 3:1–6.

60   See, for example, John 3:29, 2 Corinthians 11:2, and Revelation 19:7.

61   Matthew 11:29–30.

62   Matthew 6:24.

63   Matthew 22:37–40.

64   See, for example, 1 Corinthians 13:4–7; Ephesians 4:1–2; Colossians 3:12; 1 Timothy 6:11.

65   Galatians 5:22–23.

66   Galatians 6:1.

67   See Matthew 5:38–48.

who have been hostile—may respond by drawing closer to God, and perhaps even placing their trust in the Lord. Most of us are familiar with the proverb about heaping burning coals on an enemy's head:[68]

> If your enemy is hungry, give him food to eat; if he is thirsty, give him water to drink. In doing this, you will heap burning coals on his head, and the Lord will reward you (Prov. 25:21–22).

However, in our sinful hearts we tend to think that the burning coals[69] are a kind of punishment—a guilty conscience. But the truth is that at the time the proverb was written, there was a well-known ritual in which a repentant sinner carried burning coals on his head.[70] Thus, what the proverb is telling us is that by meekness we may be able to get our enemies to repent.

That meekness has such power was well known in the culture in which Jesus gave his Sermon on the Mount. The Roman statesman, Cato the Elder,[71] said, "Think it the first of virtues to restrain the tongue; he approaches nearest to a god who knows when it is best to be silent."[72]

The blessing promised in the third beatitude is that the meek "will inherit the earth," which, as seen above, is quoted from Old Testament Scripture. The Greek word translated as "inherit" is κληρονομεω ("klēronomeō"),[73] which literally means to "inherit" or "acquire."[74] This

---

68   Paul repeats this proverb in his letter to the Romans (Rom. 12:19–20).

69   The mineral coal is not found in Palestine, and the use of the term "coal" in Scripture typically refers to charcoal or live embers of any kind. "Coal." Merrill C. Tenney, ed., *The Zondervan Pictorial Bible Dictionary*. Grand Rapids, MI: Zondervan, 1967.

70   Robert J. Karris, ed., *Collegeville Bible Commentary: New Testament*. Collegeville, MN: The Liturgical Press, 1992. Even the prophet Isaiah says this of his own repentance: "'Woe to me!' I cried. 'I am ruined! For I am a man of unclean lips, and I live among a people of unclean lips, and my eyes have seen the King, the Lord Almighty.' Then one of the seraphs flew to me with a live coal in his hand, which he had taken with tongs from the altar. With it he touched my mouth and said, 'See, this has touched your lips; your guilt is taken away and your sin atoned for'" (Isa. 6:5–7).

71   Catherine Soanes and Angus Stevenson, ed., "Cato, Marcus Porcius," *The Oxford Dictionary of English* (revised edition). Oxford, UK: Oxford University Press, 2005. *Oxford Reference Online*. Oxford University Press. Alabama Virtual Library. 3 August 2010 <http://www.oxfordreference.com/views/ENTRY.html?subview=Main&entry=t140.e12156>.

72   In the original Latin, *"Virtutum primam esse puta compescere linguam; proximus ille deo est qui scit ratione tacere."* H. T. Riley, ed., *Dictionary of Latin Quotations, Proverbs, Maxims, and Mottos, Classical and Medieval, Including Law Terms and Phrases, With Selected Greek Quotations*. London, UK: Henry G. Bohn, 1856, 499.

73   *Strong's*, G2816; *Theology*, GK3102.

74   Ibid.

same word is used together with "blessed" and "kingdom" in describing the Great White Throne Judgment.[75] The Greek word translated as "earth" is γη[76] ("gē"), which literally means "earth" or "world."[77]

However, because the phrase "inherit the earth" is sandwiched within a body of verses the first and last of which promise the "kingdom of heaven," there is a hint that the promised land of the Old Testament has been replaced by a new promised land, a new heaven, and a new earth.[78] There can be no doubt that the "kingdom of heaven" or "kingdom of God" is an inheritance shared by Christians.[79] This inheritance, of course, includes both salvation[80] and eternal life,[81] but also much more. Jesus is the High Priest[82] and the King of Kings,[83] but we are to become priests[84] and kings[85] with Him. But the condition of our inheritance is that we surrender to God's will, which ultimately leads to suffering.[86]

75   Matthew 25:34.

76   *Strong's*, G1093; *Theology*, GK1178.

77   Ibid.

78   See 2 Peter 3:13; Revelation 21:1.

79   See Matthew 25:34; Romans 4:13; 1 Corinthians 6:9, 15:50; Galatians 3:29, 5:19–21; Hebrews 6:17; Ephesians 5:5; James 2:5.

80   Hebrews 1:14.

81   Matthew 19:29.

82   Hebrews 2:17—3:1; 4:14; 5:1–10; 6:19–20.

83   First Timothy 6:15; Revelation 17:14; 19:16.

84   Revelation 1:6; 5:9–10; 20:6.

85   Second Timothy 2:12; Revelation 2:26–27; 3:21; 5:9–10.

86   "Now if we are children, then we are heirs—heirs of God and co-heirs with Christ, if indeed we share in his sufferings in order that we may also share in his glory" (Rom. 8:17).

Questions for Further Study of the Third Beatitude

Have you ever surrendered to God? If so, did you surrender completely? Or did you surrender only part of your life to God? If so, what has kept you from surrendering completely?

How is surrender related to hope? How is it related to trust? Is it possible to surrender to God without trust?

Is surrender a one-time thing, or is it something that must be done continually? If so, have you ever noticed a difference between your life when surrendered and your life when not surrendered? Do you feel closer to God when you are surrendered? Do you feel God's power and presence in your life more strongly?

_____

_____

_____

_____

_____

_____

_____

_____

_____

_____

_____

_____

_____

_____

_____

_____

_____

_____

_____

_____

_____

_____

_____

_____

_____

When you are surrendered to God, how does that affect your relationship with others? How does it affect your view of this life? What is the natural result of surrender to God?

_____

_____

_____

_____

_____

_____

_____

_____

_____

_____

_____

_____

_____

_____

_____

_____

_____

_____

_____

_____

_____

_____

_____

_____

_____

_____

_____

_____

_____

_____

Blessed are the Meek

by Robert Leslie Palmer

Sovereign Lord, I kneel in Your presence,
Shamed by my sins and awed by Your essence.

Universal Creator, You knew me in the womb,
And blessed me, though I deserve the tomb.

Reigning King, I belong to You alone,
So now I lay myself before Your throne.

Righteous Judge, though I deserve not Your grace,
Please expunge my many sins and leave no trace.

Eternal Father, purify my soul,
And make service to You my single goal.

Nazarene, sanctify me and help me not forget,
The price You paid erased my awful debt!

Divine One, consecrate me to Your will,
And thus my life with sacred meaning fill.

Exellent Master, rule this willing slave,
Whose many sins You lovingly forgave.

Radiant Monarch, let Your glory shine,
And substitute Your will, Lord, for mine.

Our hunger and thirst for righteousness
is satisfied by God's word.

Fourth Beatitude

"Blessed are those who hunger and thirst for
righteousness, for they will be filled."

— Matthew 5:6

In the fourth beatitude, Jesus uses a metaphor of extreme hunger and
thirst to emphasize the longing for righteousness that characterizes
a person who sees that his own "righteous acts" are no more than
"filthy rags." Thus, the fourth beatitude continues the description of a
spiritual condition begun in the first beatitude and expanded in the second
and third. The Greek word translated as "hunger" is πεινάω ("peinaō"),[87]
which means to be famished almost to the point of starvation.[88] The root
of the word means to toil for daily subsistence.[89] Similarly, the Greek word
translated as "thirst" is διψάω ("dipsaō"),[90] which literally refers to physical
thirst, but was frequently used metaphorically to convey other types of
longing, particularly spiritual.[91] Thirst was very important in the arid lands
of the ancient world. Thus, the fourth beatitude emphasizes a relentless
longing for righteousness.

The choice of the terms "hunger" and "thirst" must be viewed in light
of the fact that in the Gospel of John, Jesus refers to Himself as both the
"bread of life"[92] and the "living water."[93] In so doing, Jesus echoed the
Old Testament, for in calling Himself the "bread of life," He specifically

---

87 *Strong's*, G3983; *Theology*, GK4277.
88 Ibid.
89 *Theology*, GK4293.
90 *Strong's*, G1372; *Theology*, GK1498.
91 *Theology*, GK1498.
92 John 6:35; 47–51.
93 John 4:13–14; 7:37–38.

alluded to the manna provided to the Israelites in the desert. Similarly, His references to "living water" echo the prophets Jeremiah[94] and Zechariah,[95] and similar references are made at least four times in Revelation.[96]

Not only does the fourth beatitude emphasize a longing for righteousness that characterizes a person who sees that his own "righteous acts" are no more than "filthy rags," but it also refers to precisely the kind of righteousness that such a person would expect—the righteousness to which Paul refers in Romans 3:22, righteousness from God that comes only through faith in Christ. The Greek word translated "righteousness" is δικαιοσύνη ("dikaiosunē"),[97] which literally means "uprightness,"[98] but suggests innocence or holiness. Significantly, the word is also translated as "justification."[99] This same concept of justification through faith is explained more fully in Galatians:

> We who are Jews by birth and not "Gentile sinners" know that a man is not justified by observing the law, but by faith in Jesus Christ. So we, too, have put our faith in Christ Jesus that we may be justified by faith in Christ and not by observing the law, because by observing the law no one will be justified (Gal. 2:16).

In fact, the root of "dikaiosunē" is δικαιόω (dikaioō),[100] meaning "to justify."[101] The root is used extensively in Paul's letters to make the very point that no one has ever been "righteous," and that even the Old Testament patriarchs were "credited" as righteous based on faith.[102]

Thus, in the first three beatitudes, we see a developing portrait of a sinner who realizes that he is a sinner, incapable of righteousness, who then mourns his sin and is called to repentance, and who then surrenders to God. In the fourth beatitude, the portrait develops further, for the sinner now is hungering and thirsting, not for his own righteousness, but for justification by God. And the blessing that is promised to that sinner in the fourth beatitude is to be satisfied completely. The Greek word translated

---

94 Jeremiah 2:13; 17:13.
95 Zechariah 14:8.
96 Revelation 7:17; 21:6; 22:1–2; 22:17.
97 *Strong's*, G1343; *Theology*, GK1466.
98 *Theology*, GK1466.
99 *Theology*, GK1466.
100 *Strong's*, G1344; *Theology*, GK1467.
101 Ibid.
102 See Rom. 4:2–8.

"filled" is χορτάζω ("chortazō"),[103] which literally means to "fatten" or "gorge,"[104] and the word therefore implies an abundant food supply. Thus, "chortazō" in this context means to satisfy *completely*, providing a sharp contrast to the hunger described in the first part of the fourth beatitude.

But just how are we to be filled? Just as a man dying of starvation and thirst does not permanently end his need for food and water with just one meal, the sinner who seeks justification from God must continue to feed throughout this life. Justification is an ongoing process[105] in the life of a Christian, and seeking righteousness does not end with salvation. In our daily lives, we are called on to continue seeking God's righteousness.[106] Later in the Sermon on the Mount, Jesus explains:

> Ask and it will be given to you; seek and you will find; knock and the door will be opened to you. For everyone who asks receives; he who seeks finds; and to him who knocks, the door will be opened. Which of you, if his son asks for bread, will give him a stone? Or if he asks for a fish, will give him a snake? If you, then, though you are evil, know how to give good gifts to your children, how much more will your Father in heaven give good gifts to those who ask him! (Matt. 7:7–11).

I do not agree with those who quote this Scripture as part of a "prosperity gospel," suggesting that God is a vending machine and that this Scripture is a contract obligating Him to dispense whatever we seek. Aside from the fact that different individuals may have inconsistent material prayers, it seems clear that by using the terms "bread" and "fish," Jesus is here again referring to *spiritual* gifts. First, the use of "bread" echoes the fourth beatitude itself, and therefore suggests the "bread of life." Second, because "bread" and "fish" are used together, they remind us of the miracle Jesus performed in feeding the multitude with five loaves of bread and two fish.[107] Significantly, in his Gospel, John reports that Jesus explained the spiritual significance of the miracle:

> Jesus said to them, "I tell you the truth, it is not Moses who has given you the bread from heaven, but it is my Father

---

103 *Strong's*, G5526; *Theology*, GK5963.
104 *Theology*, GK5963.
105 Second Corinthians 3:18.
106 Psalm 119:2.
107 Matthew 14:15–21; Mark 6:31–44; Luke 9:10–17; John 6:5–15.

who gives you the true bread from heaven. For the bread of God is he who comes down from heaven and gives life to the world." "Sir," they said, "from now on give us this bread." Then Jesus declared, "I am the bread of life. He who comes to me will never go hungry, and he who believes in me will never be thirsty. But as I told you, you have seen me and still you do not believe. All that the Father gives me will come to me, and whoever comes to me I will never drive away. For I have come down from heaven not to do my will but to do the will of him who sent me. And this is the will of him who sent me, that I shall lose none of all that he has given me, but raise them up at the last day. For my Father's will is that everyone who looks to the Son and believes in him shall have eternal life, and I will raise him up at the last day" (John 6:32–40).

Thus, the bread can be viewed as a symbol of *salvation*. But what of the fish? Although Jesus did not specifically refer to the fish as a metaphor in this passage, He did subsequently refer to Jonah and the "huge fish" that swallowed him as a sign that Jesus is the Messiah. When asked for a miraculous sign, Jesus told the Pharisees and teachers of the law that the only sign they would receive was Jonah's three days and three nights in the belly of a "huge fish,"[108] symbolizing the death and resurrection of Christ. The believer's baptism symbolizes exactly the same thing, and in the early church, new converts were referred to as "pisciculi," Latin for "little fishes," while the baptismal font was called the "piscina," Latin for "fishpond."[109] Indeed, a fish must be submerged under water in order to survive and is therefore an appropriate symbol of baptism.

It is possible, then, that the fish can be viewed as a symbol of *obedience*, for the first command a Christian must obey is the command to be baptized.[110] The believer, by his baptism, publicly acknowledges not only that Jesus is the risen Messiah, but also that the believer himself has died to sin.[111] Baptism, then, is a symbolic representation of the believer's commitment to obey. Thus, together, the bread and fish represent the kind

---

108 Matthew 12:38–42.
109 Jack Tresidder, *The Complete Dictionary of Symbols*. San Francisco, CA: Chronicle Books, 2004; Hans Biedermann, *Dictionary of Symbolism: Cultural Icons and the Meanings Behind Them*. Translated by James Hulbert. New York: Facts on File, 1992.
110 Matthew 28:19–20; Mark 10:39; 16:16.
111 Romans 6:1–6; Colossians 2:11–12.

of righteousness about which the fourth beatitude speaks, the justification that comes when we accept salvation and then obey the Lord.

But as stated above, justification is an ongoing process in the life of a Christian, and seeking righteousness does not end with salvation. How, then, does the Christian do that? It seems to me that to hunger and thirst for righteousness includes a strong desire to become more Christ-like, and to do so a believer must *communicate with God*. In this life we have two ways to do that—by watering our souls with prayer[112] and feeding our spirits with Bible study.[113]

Significantly, when responding to His disciples' request that He teach them how to pray, Jesus referred again to bread. In the body of the Lord's Prayer itself, Jesus included the words, "Give us each day our daily bread."[114] This might be considered solely from the material perspective, and it is good that in our prayer lives we seek no more than what we need physically. However, in light of the extensive use of bread as a spiritual metaphor throughout both the Old and New Testaments, we ought to at least consider the possibility that this is an instruction about our spiritual lives. Moreover, the context in which the petition for daily bread exists suggests a spiritual dimension, for *every* other petition in the Lord's Prayer is spiritual in nature:

- "Your kingdom come, your will be done on earth as it is in heaven."[115] These words are not merely an acknowledgment of God's sovereignty but a petition that His will be done. By seeking this daily, we add nothing to God's power but instead are asking God to help us conform our actions to His will. *To do so, we need our daily spiritual bread.*

- "Forgive us our debts, as we also have forgiven our debtors."[116] These words are not merely a petition seeking the forgiveness of our sins, but are also a

---

112 St. Teresa of Avila described prayer as water for the soul. Teresa of Ávila. *The Life of Saint Teresa of Avila by Herself.* Translated by J. M. Cohen. London, UK: Penguin Classics, 1957.

113 The metaphor of spiritually feeding on God's word appears throughout the Bible. See, for example, Deuteronomy 8:3 (quoted by Jesus in Matt. 4:4); Psalm 119:103; Isaiah 28:8; Jeremiah 15:16; Amos 8:11; Matthew 24:45; Hebrews 5:12–14; 1 Peter 2:2.

114 Luke 11:3. This is rendered as "Give us today our daily bread" in Matthew's account (Matt. 6:11).

115 Matthew 6:10.

116 Matthew 6:12.

commandment to forgive others. *To do so, we need our daily spiritual bread.*

- "And lead us not into temptation, but deliver us from the evil one."[117] These words command us not to deny that we are tempted but instead to actively confront temptation. *To do so, we need our daily spiritual bread.*

Defined simply, prayer is communication with God. And if it is God's righteousness that we seek, then why not go directly to the source? But God has also given us another way to hear His voice—through Scripture. And if it is righteousness for which we hunger and thirst, then Scripture is the knife, the fork, the spoon, the plate, and the cup.[118]

Even after we have accepted Christ as our Lord and Savior, we are still capable of sin. If we truly recognize that our own "righteousness" is no better than "filthy rags," if we mourn our own spiritual deaths, and if we have truly surrendered to God, then we will continue to hunger and thirst for His righteousness. And we know just how to satisfy our hunger and thirst, for we find God and His righteousness through prayer and studying Scripture.

---

117 Matthew 6:13.
118 Second Timothy 3:16–17.

Questions for Further Study of the Fourth Beatitude

Have you ever hungered and thirsted for God's righteousness? Do you still hunger and thirst for His righteousness? Is your hunger and thirst a daily occurrence or just an occasional occurrence?

_____

_____

_____

_____

_____

_____

_____

_____

_____

_____

_____

_____

_____

_____

_____

_____

_____

_____

_____

_____

_____

_____

_____

_____

_____

_____

_____

_____

Why did Jesus use bread and water as symbols of God's righteousness? Would the symbolism still be as effective if He had used richer food and drink as symbols? Suppose Jesus had used the modern world's junk food, say a candy bar and coke, as symbols – would they convey the same meaning?

Bread and water are staples, and they sustain life. Do you daily hunger and thirst for the bread of life and the living water, or do you merely satisfy the occasional craving for a spiritual candy bar and coke? If your hunger and thirst is not a daily occurrence, can you really claim to desire God's righteousness, His bread of life and His living water?

How would you describe your prayer life? How often do you pray? Do you pray more often in public or in private? Are your prayers to God formal and ritualistic, or are they more like conversations with a loving father? How long can you go without praying? If you don't pray, do you miss your closeness to God, or do you merely feel that you have failed to fulfill a ritual obligation?

_____

_____

_____

_____

_____

_____

_____

_____

_____

_____

_____

_____

_____

_____

_____

_____

_____

_____

_____

_____

_____

_____

_____

_____

_____

How often do you read your Bible? Do you rely on your pastor and Sunday school leaders to point you to scripture and then explain what it means, or do you read your Bible on your own? Which has more wear-and-tear – the leather or vinyl cover of your Bible, or the very thin pages? Have you ever read the entire Bible? If not, how long have you been a Christian? How many other books have you read in that same time period? When you open your Bible, do you merely read it, or do you study it?

Blessed are Those Who Hunger and Thirst for Righteousness

by Robert Leslie Palmer

My soul thirsts for communion with You, Lord,
And my spirit hungers for Your Holy Word.

On bended knee I seek to quench the drought,
So that new life my arid soul may sprout.

Ravenous spirit mine, famine's recent prey,
Now devours Your Word whenever it may.

And from living water comes the bloom,
A righteous bud that conquers tomb.

Life bestowed is nourished by the bread,
So that my spirit is daily fed.

In that new life You make another gift,
And to majestic heights my soul You lift.

That I may share Your blamelessness,
And love Your creation with holiness.

You, Creator, are source of life and growth,
And righteous bud that comes from both.

We are merciful when we allow humility
to open our hearts to love.

Fifth Beatitude

"Blessed are the merciful, for they will be shown mercy."

—Matthew 5:7

Halfway through the Beatitudes, the focus changes from those characteristics that lead to salvation and mark the new Christian to those characteristics that mark the more mature Christian. In addition, they differ in their application of the Lord's law of love,[119] for the first four beatitudes deal primarily with our love for God and our relationship with Him, while the last four focus more on our love for our neighbors and our relationships with them.[120]

The subject of the first of these new beatitudes is mercy, and yet the English word "mercy" is far more limited in its scope than its Greek counterpart. The word translated as "merciful" is ελεημων ("eleēmōn"),[121] which can just as easily refer to "compassion" as to "mercy."[122] Indeed, the word implies not just restraint in judging others, but an *active* compassion for their needs, and it is used throughout the Gospels to refer to the healing miracles Jesus performed.[123] Thus, "eleēmōn" is grounded in love for others, for one cannot be merciful without love.

---

119 Matthew 22:34–40; Mark 12:28–31.

120 This structure is similar to the Ten Commandments, the first four of which concern our relationship with God and the last six of which concern our relationship with our neighbors. See Exodus 20:2–17; Deuteronomy 5:6–21.

121 *Strong's*, G1655; *Theology*, GK1798.

122 Ibid.

123 See, for example, Matthew 9:27–31; 15:22–28; 17:15–18; Mark 5:1–20; 10:46–52; Luke 17:12–19 (translated in the NIV as "pity").

It is significant that the first beatitude that concerns Christian maturity deals with love, for love of God and neighbor is the essence of what Jesus taught:[124]

> Hearing that Jesus had silenced the Sadducees, the Pharisees got together. One of them, an expert in the law, tested him with this question: "Teacher, which is the greatest commandment in the Law?" Jesus replied: "'Love the Lord your God with all your heart and with all your soul and with all your mind.' This is the first and greatest commandment. And the second is like it: 'Love your neighbor as yourself.' All the Law and the Prophets hang on these two commandments" (Matt. 22:34–40).

Love and mercy are intertwined, for the way in which we most often show a lack of love for others is our tendency to judge and condemn them. Significantly, that tendency flows directly out of a self-righteous attitude, for if we truly see ourselves as sinners no different than any other sinners, judgment cannot be attractive. All we have to do is to think back to childhood to some incident in which we witnessed the imposition of punishment on a co-conspirator in childish mischief, for even if we had not been caught, seeing our partners in mischief punished brought only terror to our hearts. It is perhaps for this reason that Jesus specifically warned us not to judge others.[125]

The fifth beatitude says only that the merciful shall receive mercy, but Jesus repeatedly made it clear that the reverse is also true—that the unmerciful shall *not* receive mercy. In telling His disciples the parable of the unmerciful debtor, Jesus declared, "This is how my heavenly Father will treat each of you unless you forgive your brother from your heart."[126] Even in the Lord's Prayer, Jesus bids us to pray that we be forgiven to the extent that we have forgiven others.[127] And immediately after giving that model prayer to His disciples, He specifically admonished them:

> "For if you forgive men when they sin against you, your heavenly Father will also forgive you. But if you do not forgive men their sins, your Father will not forgive your sins" (Matt. 6:14–15).

---

124 See also Mark 12:28–31.
125 Matthew 7:1–5.
126 Matthew 18:35.
127 Matthew 6:12; see also James 2:12–13.

These statements made by Jesus are not declarations adding a new condition to salvation. Rather, they are plain statements recognizing that anyone who has truly accepted salvation has done so because he has acknowledged his own lack of righteousness, he has mourned his own spiritual death, and he has submitted to God's will, all as described in the first three beatitudes. Such a person will not respond to sin in another person with judgment and condemnation but rather with love and mercy. But so difficult is the lesson that even when He was being arrested, Jesus had to remind His disciples that "all who draw the sword will die by the sword."[128]

Christians, of course, are not perfect, and because our sinful nature bids us to judge and condemn, it is very difficult to avoid. As the memory of our own painful recognition of sinfulness fades and as we begin to accumulate "good works," the old self-righteous attitude invades our hearts once again. We can avoid this attitude only if we continue to hunger and thirst for righteousness, and if we continue to daily meet God through prayer and studying His word. Thus, the fifth beatitude, like those that follow, depends on the attitudes and characteristics developed in the first four beatitudes.

But when we do fail, God Himself is merciful if, after judging another, we acknowledge our sin and repent. Consider David, who judged another (and therefore himself) when the prophet Nathan confronted him with his own sin but disguised it in a parable. Instead of disputing his own harsh judgment of death, David acknowledged his sin and repented, and the Lord, speaking through Nathan, commuted the death sentence that had issued out of David's own mouth:

> Then David said to Nathan, "I have sinned against the Lord." Nathan replied, "The Lord has taken away your sin. You are not going to die. But because by doing this you have made the enemies of the Lord show utter contempt, the son born to you will die" (2 Sam. 12:13–14).

The reason mercy is so important is that God bids us to love His lost sheep. The world speaks of love, but never the kind of love about which Jesus spoke. He commanded us to love not just our families and those we like, but also our neighbors and even our enemies.[129]

---

128 Matthew 26:52.
129 Luke 6:27–38.

Thus, the mercy of which the fifth beatitude speaks is not merely mercy but compassion. And it is not merely passive but active. We are commanded to *action*, and having just been pulled up into the life raft, we cannot simply ignore the plight of fellow shipwreck victims thrashing around in the water. It is impossible to be poor in spirit, mourn our own sins, surrender to God, and then ignore the plight of our neighbors. If we do, we demonstrate that we have not had the attitude change made the subject of the first four beatitudes and that we have not surrendered to God, and for that reason, we have not received His compassion and mercy:

> "When the Son of Man comes in his glory, and all the angels with him, he will sit on his throne in heavenly glory. All the nations will be gathered before him, and he will separate the people one from another as a shepherd separates the sheep from the goats. He will put the sheep on his right and the goats on his left. Then the King will say to those on his right, 'Come, you who are blessed by my Father; take your inheritance, the kingdom prepared for you since the creation of the world. For I was hungry and you gave me something to eat, I was thirsty and you gave me something to drink, I was a stranger and you invited me in, I needed clothes and you clothed me, I was sick and you looked after me, I was in prison and you came to visit me.' Then the righteous will answer him, 'Lord, when did we see you hungry and feed you, or thirsty and give you something to drink? When did we see you a stranger and invite you in, or needing clothes and clothe you? When did we see you sick or in prison and go to visit you?' The King will reply, 'I tell you the truth, whatever you did for one of the least of these brothers of mine, you did for me.' Then he will say to those on his left, 'Depart from me, you who are cursed, into the eternal fire prepared for the devil and his angels. For I was hungry and you gave me nothing to eat, I was thirsty and you gave me nothing to drink, I was a stranger and you did not invite me in, I needed clothes and you did not clothe me, I was sick and in prison and you did not look after me.' They also will answer, 'Lord, when did we see you hungry or thirsty or a stranger or needing clothes or sick

or in prison, and did not help you?' He will reply, 'I tell you the truth, whatever you did not do for one of the least of these, you did not do for me.' Then they will go away to eternal punishment, but the righteous to eternal life'" (Matt. 25:31–46).

Mercy and compassion are therefore the first fruits that begin flowering in the life of a maturing Christian.

Questions for Further Study of the Fifth Beatitude

How is the first Beatitude related to the fifth? How is humility related to compassion? Is it possible to show true compassion in the absence of humility?

_____

_____

_____

_____

_____

_____

_____

_____

_____

_____

_____

_____

_____

_____

_____

_____

_____

_____

_____

_____

_____

_____

_____

Do you have compassion for others? If so, are you always compassionate?
Have you ever been unmerciful? In what circumstances do you think you
are most compassionate? In what circumstances do you think that you
are least compassionate? What can you do to increase your capacity for
compassion?

Do you find it difficult to forgive others? If so, why? Have you ever been able to forgive for other than minor offenses? If so, what gave you the strength to forgive in those circumstances? What can you do to increase your capacity to forgive?

_____

_____

_____

_____

_____

_____

_____

_____

_____

_____

_____

_____

_____

_____

_____

_____

_____

_____

_____

_____

_____

_____

_____

_____

_____

Blessed are the Merciful

by Robert Leslie Palmer

Can I seek vengeance for my neighbor's sin
While hoping for me Your mercy to win?

Oh, cleanse my heart that I forgive,
And help my debtors repent and live.

Make me like You, help me embrace
All Your people, so they find grace.

Place in my heart sublime desire,
Concern for others that will not tire.

Accept the gifts now fully tendered
Of heart and soul and mind surrendered.

Spend these gifts as You ordain
That wayward sheep You might regain.

Supply my spirit with holy grace,
That helps lost sinners seek Your face.

Instill in me Your holy, gentle trait,
So I regard with love and not in hate.

On the cross You nailed transgression,
That all may live who make confession.

Now, my Lord, I know I must
Love my foes so You they trust.

We are pure in heart when we value
lost sinners as Jesus does.

Sixth Beatitude

"Blessed are the pure in heart, for they will see God."

—Matthew 5:8

The sixth beatitude concerns another quality of the maturing believer, purity of heart. The Greek word translated as "pure" is καθαρος ("katharos"),[130] from which we get our English word "catharsis." "Katharos" literally means "clean" or "pure,"[131] and therefore echoes the ritual cleanliness of the Law of Moses, though as a contrast. The word translated as "heart" is καρδια ("kardia"),[132] from which we get our English words "cardiac" and "cardiology." "Kardia" literally refers to the physical heart, but just as in English, it is figuratively used to refer to the mind, one's thoughts and feelings, the part of each of us to which God speaks.[133] Thus, to be pure in heart suggests that our innermost beings, our souls, be clean and pure. But is this purity even possible for beings whose "righteousness" is no cleaner than the "filthy rags" to which the prophet Isaiah refers?

The answer is a resounding no, for Scripture is clear that we cannot, in our natural state, ever be pure in heart.[134] In fact, our hearts are the very source of our evil. In pointing out that the Pharisees were exalting ritual over faith and form over substance, Jesus warned:[135]

---

130 *Strong's*, G2513; *Theology*, GK2754.

131 Ibid.

132 *Strong's*, G2588; *Theology*, GK2840.

133 Ibid.

134 Genesis 6:5; Psalm 64:6; Proverbs 20:9; Jeremiah 17:9. Of course, as Christians we have a righteousness imputed from God. Romans 3:20-24.

135 See also Mark 7:21–23.

"Don't you see that whatever enters the mouth goes into the stomach and then out of the body? But the things that come out of the mouth come from the heart, and these make a man 'unclean.' For out of the heart come evil thoughts, murder, adultery, sexual immorality, theft, false testimony, slander. These are what make a man 'unclean;' but eating with unwashed hands does not make him 'unclean'" (Matt. 15:17–20).

Jesus repeatedly made the point that ritual cleanliness was not enough. The Old Testament laws about ritual cleanliness were very detailed and very complex, and they prohibited things that to modern sensibilities seem strange. For example, one such law dictated that during her menstrual period, a woman was ceremonially unclean, and that anyone or anything that touched her was also ceremonially unclean.[136] We should always bear this in mind when we contemplate our own "righteousness," which, as explained above, the prophet Isaiah compared to the "filthy rags" used as the biblical equivalent of a tampon.

But Jesus was not exalting the kind of ritual purity or ceremonial cleanliness touted by the Pharisees. Instead, Jesus taught that compassion is far more important than ritual, a lesson made very clear in the parable of the Good Samaritan.[137] In reading this parable two thousand years later, in a country and culture far removed from that in which Jesus spoke, we risk missing key points if we do not read the parable carefully. First, we are told that the "expert in the law" to whom Jesus told the parable was looking to *justify* himself. This tells us that Jesus knew that the "expert" had not yet even reached the attitude that was the subject of the first beatitude, for if he had, he would have known that his goal was impossible. Second, Jesus knew that even though the "expert in the law" knew that love for God and neighbor was paramount, as indicated by his answer to the questions Jesus asked, he was nevertheless looking to Old Testament law as the tool with which he would justify himself. Thus, Jesus gave this "expert" a parable in which he had to make a choice between compassion and Old Testament ritual law. That is why Jesus described the robbery victim as half dead, for anyone who touched a dead body was ceremonially defiled and could not participate in worship at the temple.[138] Then, Jesus describes the first two

---

136 Leviticus 15:19–30.
137 Luke 10:25–37.
138 Numbers 19:13.

persons—the ones who did nothing for the robbery victim—as a priest and a Levite, two religious figures. By walking to the other side of the road, they were deliberately choosing to exalt form over substance and ritual over compassion.

The parable of the Good Samaritan teaches much about how we must respond to the needs of our neighbors, but we can take it further if we think of the robbery victim in a spiritual sense, for we are called not just to minister to our neighbors' physical needs but also to their spiritual needs. Thus, if we take the robbery victim as a symbol of an unbeliever, a person who is already "half dead" because he remains spiritually dead, then what does the parable say about the choices we make every day between ritual worship and compassion for sinners?

But we don't even make a serious effort to meet the physical needs of the suffering, much less the spiritual. A simple review of many church budgets today reveals the astonishing fact that the amount allocated to actually ministering to the needs of others almost always pales in comparison to every other budget category, from ministerial salaries to the erection and maintenance of facilities and grounds! In contrast, the apostle Paul worked to support himself[139] and the early church met in the homes of believers,[140] with the result that money collected was actually used to minister to others.[141] Then the church was viewed as a fellowship of believers called to action; now the church has been relegated to the status of a service industry: professional ministers cater to the needs of "members" and no one gives much thought at all to the suffering world outside the church, except to criticize it. If we truly want to be "pure in heart," we must open our hearts to both the physical and spiritual needs of the suffering all around us.

The promise made in the sixth beatitude is that the "pure in heart" will "see God." We know from Scripture that we cannot see God in our natural, sinful condition,[142] and that unbelievers cannot see God because their hearts are "calloused."[143] This is because as sinners we live in darkness while God lives in "unapproachable light, whom no one has seen or can see."[144] At one time or another, all of us have suddenly walked from darkness into a well-lit room, and we could not see because our eyes had to adjust. If,

---

139 Acts 18:1–3, 20:33–34; 1 Corinthians 9:12.
140 Acts 20:20; Romans 16:5; 1 Corinthians 16:19; Colossians 4:15; Philemon 1:2.
141 See, for example, Romans 15:26.
142 Exodus 33:20; John 1:18; 6:46; Hebrews 12:14.
143 Matthew 13:13–16. See also Mark 4:11–12 and John 9:39–41.
144 First Timothy 6:16.

as believers, we do not move out of the darkness in which we lived before we were believers, we can never expect to see anything remarkable. This brings us to what Jesus meant when He said that the "pure in heart" will "see God."

The Greek word translated as "God" is θεος ("theos"),[145] from which we get our English word "theology." "Theos" can refer to any so-called deity, but generally refers to the Supreme Divinity.[146] The Greek word translated as "see" is οπτανομαι ("optanomai"),[147] from which we get our English words "optics" and "optical." "Optanomai" literally means to stare with eyes wide open, as if looking at something remarkable.[148] It is a very specific meaning, for there are at least five Greek words that can be translated as "see," and all of them have very distinct meanings. By understanding the distinctions made in Greek, we can better understand the specific word used in the sixth beatitude.

- The Greek word βλεπω ("blepo")[149] denotes simple observation.[150]

- The Greek word ειδω ("eido")[151] refers to passive or casual vision or perception.[152]

- The Greek word θεαομαι ("theaomai")[153] signifies continuing inspection.[154]

- The Greek word σκοπεω or ("skopeo")[155] refers to watching from a distance, as in aiming a weapon or spying.[156]

Thus, the picture we get is of a person not simply observing God or inspecting Him or spying on Him from a distance. Instead, the use of the word "optanomai" tells us that if we mature in the faith and become "pure

---

145 *Strong's*, G2316; *Theology*, GK2536.
146 Ibid.
147 *Strong's*, G3700; *Theology*, GK3964. In *Theology*, the word is found by looking at its root, ὁράω ("horaō"), GK3972.
148 *Strong's-QuickVerse.*
149 *Strong's*, G991.
150 Ibid.
151 *Strong's*, G1492.
152 Ibid.
153 *Strong's*, G2300.
154 Ibid.
155 *Strong's*, G4648.
156 Ibid.

in heart," what we see will be so remarkable that we will stare with our eyes wide open. First, it is clear that believers will actually see God face to face after resurrection.[157] But I believe that the sixth beatitude is telling us more, that we can see God in this life, if we will but open our eyes. Even the act of faith itself involves this kind of "holy" vision:

> Then Jesus cried out, "When a man believes in me, he does not believe in me only, but in the one who sent me. When he looks at me, he sees the one who sent me" (John 12:44–45).

What this tells us is that if we will but have simple faith and place our trust in Christ, if we will but open our eyes, we will see remarkable things. Just as we see the wind through the movement of leaves and grass, we see God through His miracles. When we mature in faith, we can see the evidence of God all around us, even in other believers. But more than that, by trusting God, we change our focus from the external and superficial to the internal and profound, and we thereby begin to see as God does:

> The Lord does not look at the things man looks at. Man looks at the outward appearance, but the Lord looks at the heart (1 Sam. 16:7).

Thus, the more that we allow God to purify our hearts as we trust Him, the more that our vision will be sharpened so that we begin to focus on the things of the heart rather than on the things of this world. That means that the way we look at others, both believers and unbelievers, will change. First, our ability to distinguish between believers and unbelievers—between the wheat and the tares[158]—will increase. Second, our sensitivity to the needs of our brothers and sisters in Christ will increase. And finally, our ability to see the unbelievers ready for God's word will increase.

My favorite musical is *Man of La Mancha*, in which the entire story is concerned with the manner in which we see the world and the people in it. The principal character is Don Quixote, a crazy old man tired of the world and its deceit and debauchery. When he can no longer tolerate the world, he dons armor and declares himself to be a knight on a quest. From then on he sees everything with very different eyes. He stops at an inn that he perceives to be a castle, he proclaims his love for a "lady" who is only

---

157 Psalm 17:15; Revelation 22:3–4.
158 There are unbelievers intermingled with believers in every congregation. See Matthew 13:24–30.

a prostitute, and he jousts with a windmill, perceiving it to be a dragon. In many ways, he is not unlike the immature Christian who thinks that his mission is some glorious quest. But in the end, the effect he has on those around him has nothing to do with his silly quest but rather with the compassion he shows for the prostitute, Aldonza. That he sees her in a manner different than others do is highlighted by the fact that he calls her by another name, Dulcinea, and of all the things that he has "seen" with different eyes, his vision of her is most correct, for he sees her as God would. Although a prostitute, she is poor in spirit and ready for change.

But it is precisely because Don Quixote has seen Aldonza in a different light, as having value, that she ultimately repents. His altered vision has changed his actions so that he shows her a compassion she has never seen, a compassion that makes her mourn her own sin. Christians would be well advised to seek to see others as God does when engaged in evangelism, for the truth is that unbelievers do not respond well to condemnation. But when we show compassion, as Jesus did, we sow seeds that lead to spiritual mourning and surrender.

Man of La Mancha is just a play, but it illustrates what I believe the sixth beatitude is telling us. When we are poor in spirit, mourn our sins, surrender to God, and hunger and thirst for His righteousness, then we will mature in our faith and our eyes will be opened. In the future, we will see God in heaven, and now we will see Him in His creation and His miracles. But in addition, instead of seeing other sinners, particularly unbelievers, as people to be despised, we will begin to see them as belonging to God, as having value, and our actions toward them will change profoundly.

Questions for Further Study of the Sixth Beatitude

How is the second Beatitude related to the sixth? How is mourning related to purity of heart? Is it possible to be pure in heart without first mourning one's own sins?

Have you ever clearly seen evidence of God's work in your own life? Have you ever seen such evidence in the lives of others? What made you believe that what you saw was God's work?

Have you ever had an experience that you could describe as stepping out of darkness into light? If so, what was the source of the light? Did you remain in the light, or did you slide back into the darkness?

_____

_____

_____

_____

_____

_____

_____

_____

_____

_____

_____

_____

_____

_____

_____

_____

_____

_____

_____

_____

_____

_____

_____

_____

_____

_____

_____

_____

_____

Blessed are the Pure in Heart

by Robert Leslie Palmer

Purge my soul, Lord, and cleanse my mind,
Because my sin has made me blind.

Unable to look upon Your semblance,
Now I stumble toward Your presence.

Reaching out, as blind men always must,
I seek Your hand, a hand that all may trust.

Is this the reason You snatched my sight,
That I might learn I need Your light?

Then expel my sin, and set me free,
So that again Your face I'll see!

You, my God, make wrong hearts right,
And doing that, restore lost sight.

We know peace when we trust our Heavenly
Father as an infant trusts his own father.

Seventh Beatitude

"Blessed are the peacemakers, for they will be called sons of God."

—Matthew 5:9

In the seventh beatitude, the Greek word translated as "peacemaker" is ειρηνοποιος ("eirēnopoios").[159] It appears only twice in the entire New Testament, in the seventh beatitude and again in James, and there appears to be no Hebrew equivalent in the Old Testament. However, the root word for "peace," ειρηνη ("eirēnē"),[160] appears ninety-two times in the New Testament and in its purest (classical) sense refers primarily to the absence of war rather than to a spiritual state.[161] But by the time the New Testament was written, the meaning of the word had broadened to include the concepts of spiritual peace and wholeness or unity.[162] "Peacemaker" or "eirēnopoios" therefore suggests not only promotion of peace but also wholeness and unity, both in the spirit and in the church.

We know that God first made peace with sinful man. Isaiah prophesied that peace.[163] At Christ's birth, angels declared that peace.[164] Before his death, Jesus told his disciples that he was leaving them with His peace.[165] And when Jesus died, the curtain in the temple was torn in two from top

---

159 *Strong's*, G1518; *Theology*, GK 1648.
160 *Strong's*, G1515; *Theology*, GK 1645.
161 *Theology*, GK 1645.
162 *Strong's*, G1515; *Theology*, GK 1645.
163 Isaiah 9:6.
164 Luke 2:14.
165 John 14:27.

to bottom,[166] signifying that God had removed the barrier that man's sin had erected and had thereby reconciled man to Himself.[167]

After the resurrection, the apostles finally understood that God had been the peacemaker, reconciling sinful mankind to Himself,[168] and that we are now called to become peacemakers ourselves—"Christ's ambassadors" in a "ministry of reconciliation."[169] But just what is this ministry of reconciliation, and what does it mean to be a peacemaker? I believe that it involves at least three parts. First, we are called to be peacemakers with ourselves, for even as Christians, we continue to wage war with our own sinful nature and lack the unity or wholeness that come with true peace:

> I know that nothing good lives in me, that is, in my sinful nature. For I have the desire to do what is good, but I cannot carry it out. For what I do is not the good I want to do; no, the evil I do not want to do—this I keep on doing. Now if I do what I do not want to do, it is no longer I who do it, but it is sin living in me that does it. So I find this law at work: When I want to do good, evil is right there with me. For in my inner being I delight in God's law; but I see another law at work in the members of my body, waging war against the law of my mind and making me a prisoner of the law of sin at work within my members. What a wretched man I am! Who will rescue me from this body of death? Thanks be to God—through Jesus Christ our Lord! So then, I myself in my mind am a slave to God's law, but in the sinful nature a slave to the law of sin (Rom. 7:18–25).

The new Christian finds this inner war particularly difficult, and sometimes the older Christian who has not matured simply learns how to ignore the war, with disastrous consequences, for in so doing, he makes himself vulnerable to sin. But the maturing Christian learns over time that the more he surrenders to God and yields to the guidance of the Holy Spirit, the less intense the inner war, for he gradually achieves a

---

166 Matthew 27:51.
167 Ephesians 2:13–18.
168 Romans 5:1–2; Romans 5:10.
169 Second Corinthians 5:17–20.

measure of victory over his sinful nature.[170] Mastery of this simple concept is so important that we have no hope of success in the other parts of the reconciliation ministry if we cannot achieve peace within ourselves.

Second, we are called to be peacemakers within the church.[171] The fact that the modern church is so full of division and controversy is a sad testament to the lack of maturity among present believers, at least in America. For some reason, we find it more satisfying to debate minor theological points and to engage in protracted doctrinal disputes than to simply yield to God and promote peace with our brothers and sisters in Christ. That so much division exists in the church today also evidences our failure to truly recognize that our own righteousness is no better than "filthy rags," for if we truly recognized that fact, we would have less interest in the minor doctrines upon which we rely to "justify" ourselves, and we would therefore be less likely to take offense at the actions of a fellow believer. But even if the other believer has truly done something that must be addressed, Jesus told us precisely how to approach him:

> "If your brother sins against you, go and show him his fault, just between the two of you. If he listens to you, you have won your brother over. But if he will not listen, take one or two others along, so that 'every matter may be established by the testimony of two or three witnesses.' If he refuses to listen to them, tell it to the church; and if he refuses to listen even to the church, treat him as you would a pagan or a tax collector" (Matt. 18:15–17).

But we ignore this instruction, and the modern church is without peace. This failure is very aptly described in John Godfrey Saxe's poem, "Six Blind Men and the Elephant."[172] In the poem, Saxe describes a dispute among six blind men who have examined an elephant, each grasping a part of the elephant and describing it accurately. Knowing that his own description is accurate, each man argues "loud and long" but fails to realize that he only has part of the truth and that the others are just as accurate

---

170 "The mind of sinful man is death, but the mind controlled by the Spirit is life and peace" (Rom. 8:6); "For if you live according to the sinful nature, you will die; but if by the Spirit you put to death the misdeeds of the body, you will live, because those who are led by the Spirit of God are sons of God. For you did not receive a spirit that makes you a slave again to fear, but you received the Spirit of sonship. And by him we cry, 'Abba, Father'" (Rom. 8:13–15).

171 First Thessalonians 5:13; Ephesians 4:3.

172 Hazel Felleman, *The Best Loved Poems of the American People*. New York: Doubleday, 1936. The poem can be found in many anthologies.

in their descriptions. Then Saxe concludes his poem with a declaration that the disputants in theological wars are like these blind men, not one of whom has actually seen the "elephant" (i.e., God). This, of course, is the very subject of the sixth beatitude. Thus, without the purity of heart described in that beatitude, it is not possible to become the peacemaker contemplated in the seventh beatitude.

Finally, we are called to be peacemakers within the communities in which we live.[173] This seems to be a difficult concept for the modern Christian, for as discussed above, we remain self-righteous and are therefore inclined to judge unbelievers. In so doing, all but a few fail to take advantage of one of the most potent evangelism tools we have, for "Peacemakers who sow in peace raise a harvest of righteousness."[174] Jesus understood this and seemed to reserve public condemnation and judgment solely for the ecclesiastical insiders, the self-righteous. *Indeed, I can find no example of Jesus condemning anyone else.* And the manner in which He dealt with the adulterous woman is a powerful example of this concept:

> The teachers of the law and the Pharisees brought in a woman caught in adultery. They made her stand before the group and said to Jesus, "Teacher, this woman was caught in the act of adultery. In the Law Moses commanded us to stone such women. Now what do you say?" They were using this question as a trap, in order to have a basis for accusing him. But Jesus bent down and started to write on the ground with his finger. When they kept on questioning him, he straightened up and said to them, "If any one of you is without sin, let him be the first to throw a stone at her." Again he stooped down and wrote on the ground. At this, those who heard began to go away one at a time, the older ones first, until only Jesus was left, with the woman still standing there. Jesus straightened up and asked her, "Woman, where are they? Has no one condemned you?" "No one, sir," she said. "Then neither do I condemn you," Jesus declared. "Go now and leave your life of sin" (John 8:3–11).

---

173 Romans 12:18.
174 James 3:18. This is the only other time that the word "peacemakers" appears in the Bible.

Note first that Jesus made peace between the adulterous woman and her accusers by making them think of their own sinful natures—by making them directly confront their self-righteousness. Then, when He alone was qualified to condemn her, for He alone was without sin, He deliberately chose *not* to condemn her, even though it is not reported that she sought forgiveness. Instead, by saving her from stoning and refusing to condemn her, He demonstrated incredible compassion. And that was what made His final admonition to her—"Go now and leave your life of sin"—so powerful. Contrast this to the modern Christian standing on the street corner self-righteously condemning "sinners" and telling perfect strangers they are destined for hell. Which is the more powerful evangelistic technique?

I am not suggesting that God's truth be compromised or that sin be tolerated, but only that there is a proper time and way to help unbelievers confront their own sin. It is *never* our place to judge others, and until we have developed a relationship with an unbeliever, anything we say about his sin will be considered (and may well be) self-righteous. Of course, to develop a relationship requires a commitment of time, energy, resources, and most of all, *love*. And to help someone confront sin in his own life has an additional requirement—that the work of the Holy Spirit be evident in our own lives. Otherwise nothing we do or say will be of help to the other sinner. Often we modern Christians fear and avoid the commitment of time, energy, resources, and love that is required, and we know deep in our hearts that the work of the Holy Spirit is frustrated in our own lives. That, I believe, is why we seek anonymity in our evangelistic efforts.

To understand this concept better, we must examine the second part of the seventh beatitude, the blessing of which it speaks. The Greek words translated as "called" and "God" have been discussed above in connection with the second and sixth beatitudes, respectively. The Greek word translated as "son" is υιος ("huios"),[175] which literally means "son," but could be used for any immediate kinsman.[176] God first promised to make the nation of Israel His sons,[177] but later extended that promise to those who accept Christ as their savior.[178] Jesus explained that the true sons of God love Him and *hear* what He has to say:

---

175 *Strong's*, G5207; *Theology*, GK 5626.
176 Ibid.
177 Hosea 1:10.
178 Romans 9:25–26; Galatians 3:26–27.

Jesus said to them, "If God were your Father, you would love me, for I came from God and now am here. I have not come on my own; but he sent me. Why is my language not clear to you? Because you are unable to hear what I say. You belong to your father, the devil, and you want to carry out your father's desire. He was a murderer from the beginning, not holding to the truth, for there is no truth in him. When he lies, he speaks his native language, for he is a liar and the father of lies. Yet because I tell the truth, you do not believe me! Can any of you prove me guilty of sin? If I am telling the truth, why don't you believe me? He who belongs to God hears what God says. The reason you do not hear is that you do not belong to God" (John 8:42–47).

We do not listen to God—because we are not truly sons of God—if we do not listen to the Holy Spirit.[179]

This takes us right back to the inner war, the war with our own sinful natures. To be sons of God, we must listen to the Holy Spirit and not our own sinful natures. If we do that, we are truly sons of God, and will therefore share in the inheritance[180] and become priest-kings together with Christ.

---

179 Romans 8:13–15.
180 Galatians 4:1–8. See also Romans 8:16–17 and Ephesians 1:3–6.

Questions for Further Study of the Seventh Beatitude

How is the third Beatitude related to the seventh? How is surrender related to peace? Is it possible to have true peace in the absence of surrender to God?

_____

_____

_____

_____

_____

_____

_____

_____

_____

_____

_____

_____

_____

_____

_____

_____

_____

_____

_____

_____

_____

_____

_____

_____

_____

Have you ever been truly at peace in your heart? If so, what was the source of that peace? What was your attitude toward God when you felt that peace? Have you remained at peace? If not, why not?

_____

_____

_____

_____

_____

_____

_____

_____

_____

_____

_____

_____

_____

_____

_____

_____

_____

_____

_____

_____

_____

_____

_____

_____

_____

_____

_____

_____

_____

_____

Has your church ever been involved in a divisive conflict? If so, what was the source of the trouble? How did the church leaders handle the conflict? What was the end result of the conflict? Do you think that God would have approved of the manner in which the conflict was resolved? If not, why not?

_____

_____

_____

_____

_____

_____

_____

_____

_____

_____

_____

_____

_____

_____

_____

_____

_____

_____

_____

_____

_____

_____

_____

_____

_____

_____

_____

_____

Have you ever been a "peacemaker" with unbelievers? How do you reach out to unbelievers? Is your evangelism anonymous, or do you take the time to know the unbelievers you are trying to reach? Do you address their physical and material needs, or do you just preach the gospel? Are you more concerned with statistical "conversions" or actually loving the lost?

_____

_____

_____

_____

_____

_____

_____

_____

_____

_____

_____

_____

_____

_____

_____

_____

_____

_____

_____

_____

_____

_____

_____

_____

Blessed are the Peacemakers

by Robert Leslie Palmer

Power seduces at an early age,
And exacts from each a fearful wage.

Experience proves our control a farce,
And attempts to govern our peace does parse.

Amity escapes us, accord is lost,
The illusion of power has an awful cost.

Conflict dominates this earthly realm,
And will so long as we command the helm.

Ending the strife is within our control,
If we surrender fully our heart and soul.

We know that we are maturing Christians
when we are persecuted for righteousness.

Eighth Beatitude

"Blessed are those who are persecuted because of
righteousness, for theirs is the kingdom of heaven."

—Matthew 5:10

Jesus concludes His introduction to the Sermon on the Mount with
a promise identical to the one found in the very first beatitude. In
the first beatitude, the kingdom of heaven is promised to the "poor
in spirit." In the final beatitude, the kingdom of heaven is promised to
those persecuted for righteousness. As stated above, I have concluded
that this is a poetic device suggesting that the kingdom of heaven is the
subject of all of the Beatitudes, and, indeed, of the Sermon on the Mount,
which the Beatitudes introduce. Because it is such an important topic,
the kingdom of heaven is discussed in a separate section below, and this
section will concern itself with the Christian attribute covered by the
eighth beatitude—persecution for righteousness.

The Greek word translated as "righteousness" is the same word used
in the fourth beatitude, discussed above, and the word translated as
"persecuted" is διωκω ("diōkō"),[181] which literally means to zealously
"chase," "pursue," "drive away," or "hunt."[182] "Diōkō" is found forty-five
times in the New Testament, which immediately suggests that persecution
is simply a part of being a Christian, a follower of Christ:

- Jesus Himself was persecuted for righteousness, for He
  was stripped, flogged, mocked, and crucified.[183] This

---

181 *Strong's*, G1377; *Theology*, GK 1503.
182 Ibid.
183 Matthew 26:47—27:50; Mark 14:43—15:37; Luke 22:47—23:46; John 18:3—19:30.

happened even though Jesus was innocent,[184] a fact recognized even by Judas, His betrayer,[185] and Pilate, His judge.[186] Even the centurion overseeing the execution declared Jesus to be a "righteous man."[187] Despite the injustice, His dying prayer was "Father, forgive them, for they do not know what they are doing."[188] Significantly, it was the *religious authorities* who persecuted Jesus, for they instigated the arrest, rigged trial, and execution.[189]

- Stephen, the first Christian martyr, was initially opposed by members of the Synagogue of the Freedmen, who stirred up the elders and teachers of the law, after which he was tried on false testimony before the Sanhedrin and ultimately stoned to death.[190] As he died, he prayed, "Lord, do not hold this sin against them."[191] Once again, it was the *religious authorities* who were responsible for the persecution. Among them was the apostle Paul,[192] who was a Pharisee before his conversion.[193]

- Although it is not recorded in Scripture, the traditional view is that Paul was beheaded.[194] During his ministry, he rejoiced in persecution,[195] and even when he was warned that arrest was imminent, he responded, "I am ready not only to be bound, but also to die in Jerusalem for the name of the Lord Jesus."[196] Again, with no little irony, it was the *religious authorities* who persecuted Paul.[197]

---

184 Hebrews 4:15.
185 Matthew 27:4.
186 Matthew 27:19; Luke 23:4.
187 Luke 23:47.
188 Luke 23:34.
189 Matthew 12:14; 26:4; Mark 3:6; John 5:16, 11:53.
190 Acts 6:8—7:60.
191 Acts 7:60.
192 Acts 7:58.
193 Philippians 3:5.
194 Due to Paul's Roman citizenship, he was entitled to beheading, which was considered a more merciful execution. Bentley, James, *A Calendar of Saints: The Lives of the Principal Saints of the Christian Year*. New York: Facts on File, 1986.
195 First Corinthians 4:11–13; 2 Corinthians 4:8–12, 6:4–10, 11:24–27, 12:9–10; Galatians 5:11; 1 Thessalonians 2:2, 3:4.
196 Acts 21:13.
197 Eusebius, *History of the Church II*, 25:5.

- As with Paul, although it is not recorded in Scripture, the traditional view is that Peter died as a martyr in Rome, crucified upside down at his own request because he did not feel worthy to die in the same way Jesus had.[198]

- James, the brother of John, was put to death by the sword at the order of King Herod.[199]

These are just a few examples, and so we should not be surprised by persecution. Indeed, Jesus specifically told us that we would be persecuted:

> "I am sending you out like sheep among wolves. Therefore be as shrewd as snakes and as innocent as doves. Be on your guard against men; they will hand you over to the local councils and flog you in their synagogues. On my account you will be brought before governors and kings as witnesses to them and to the Gentiles. But when they arrest you, do not worry about what to say or how to say it. At that time you will be given what to say, for it will not be you speaking, but the Spirit of your Father speaking through you" (Matt. 10:16–20).

There are at least two significant things about this statement. First, Jesus did not say "a few of you" or "some of you" or even "many of you" will be persecuted, but rather simply "you" will be persecuted. On another occasion, Jesus reiterated this point, saying, "If they persecuted me, they will persecute you also."[200] That He was speaking in the plural is clear from the original Greek and was understood even at the writing of the King James translation. Unfortunately, modern English fails to adequately serve the reader, for today "you" is both singular and plural. But the King James translation was written when the distinction between the plural "you" and "ye" and the singular "thou" and "thee" had not yet been lost, and, consistent with the original Greek, the King James translation uses only

---

198 James Bentley, *A Calendar of Saints: The Lives of the Principal Saints of the Christian Year.* New York: Facts on File, 1986; Eusebius, *History of the Church II*, 25:5; First Epistle of Clement to the Corinthians 5:4. Tradition also holds that Peter was crucified at the Circus of Nero, where the Vatican now stands. Reader's Digest Association, *Who's Who in the Bible.* Pleasantville, New York: The Reader's Digest Association, 1994.

199 Acts 12:2.

200 John 15:20.

the plural form of the second person pronoun in these verses. Thus, Jesus was telling us that we should *all* expect persecution if we are obedient to Him.

The second significant point in the warning of persecution found in Matthew 10 is that Jesus described for us a specific pattern of persecution that begins with the *religious authorities*. The architect of persecution is Satan, and although it may seem that he would choose to persecute believers primarily from outside the church, that would be a strategic mistake. Opposition from outside a group tends to create unity within the group, but opposition from within, especially from those in authority, tends to divide a group. Thus, strategically, it makes more sense to stir up dissension within the body of believers. To do so, of course, requires the infiltration of that body. But that is precisely what we are to expect, for Jesus warned us about the tares among the wheat[201] and about false prophets,[202] and we would do well to heed His warnings. Indeed, this very point is made clear in the two verses that follow and expand the eighth beatitude:

> "Blessed are you when people insult you, persecute you and falsely say all kinds of evil against you because of me. Rejoice and be glad, because great is your reward in heaven, for in the same way they persecuted the prophets who were before you" (Matt. 5:11–12).

By referring to the prophets, Jesus was once again pointing to persecution that comes from the recognized *religious authorities*, for they were the ones who persecuted the prophets.

For some reason, when talking about persecution today, Christians tend to think primarily of the unbelieving world rather than the religious authorities. In support of this concept, Christians point to the involvement of the civil authorities of Rome in the persecution of early believers. To be sure, the Roman government was often involved, but in instance after instance in the New Testament we are told that the civil authorities were stirred to action by religious leaders. Unfortunately, that fact is often lost because those leaders are often referred to simply as the "Jews,"[203] which has caused some to warp those same Scriptures into justification for anti-Semitism and even persecution of Jews. It is ironic that Scriptures written

201 Matthew 13:24–30, 38–42.
202 Matthew 7:15–16, 24:10–11, 24:24; Mark 13:22.
203 See, for example, John 5:16-18; Acts 9:22–24.

to *condemn* religious persecution have themselves been transmogrified into an *excuse* for religious persecution!

Unfortunately, many professing Christians, embarrassed by what these Scriptures *seem* to say, simply ignore them. That is a big mistake, for they have much to say, and it is not a lesson in anti-Semitism. That universal condemnation of Jews was not intended should be clear to any serious student of the Bible. First, there is no doubt that Jesus was a Jew, and Matthew goes to great pains to trace the genealogy of Jesus back through King David to Abraham.[204] Indeed, much of what is described in the New Testament took place in Judea, and so it is only natural that the principal players are all Jewish.

Second, Jesus declared that "salvation is from the Jews."[205] The first Christians were all Jews, including the apostles, and when the Gentiles began to believe, they felt gratitude rather than hatred toward Jews and even took up offerings to relieve suffering among the Jews:

> They were pleased to do it, and indeed they owe it to them. For if the Gentiles have shared in the Jews' spiritual blessings, they owe it to the Jews to share with them their material blessings (Rom. 15:27).

Indeed, Scripture tells us that there is no difference between Jew and Gentile:

> What shall we conclude then? Are we any better? Not at all! We have already made the charge that Jews and Gentiles alike are all under sin (Rom. 3:9).

But perhaps most important of all is the lesson to be drawn from the life of the apostle Paul. Before he became a believer, he was among the Jewish religious leadership that persecuted the early Christians:[206]

> For you have heard of my previous way of life in Judaism, how intensely I persecuted the church of God and tried

---

204 Matthew 1:1–16.

205 John 4:22.

206 Paul confessed this fact repeatedly, not just in his epistle to the Galatians. "'Lord,' I replied, 'these men know that I went from one synagogue to another to imprison and beat those who believe in you. And when the blood of your martyr Stephen was shed, I stood there giving my approval and guarding the clothes of those who were killing him'" (Acts 22:19–20). "For I am the least of the apostles and do not even deserve to be called an apostle, because I persecuted the church of God" (1 Cor. 15:9).

to destroy it. I was advancing in Judaism beyond many Jews of my own age and was extremely zealous for the traditions of my fathers (Gal. 1:13–14).

Known as Saul before his conversion,[207] Paul was on the road to Damascus when he encountered the risen Christ, who asked, "Saul, Saul, why do you persecute me?"[208] He repented, became a believer, and ultimately was persecuted himself, as described above.

Repenting did not alter the fact that Paul was a Jew, but it did change his status as a self-righteous Pharisee. Thus, if the quality that is condemned is that of being Jewish, then Paul would not be so highly regarded by Christians today. Instead, we must conclude that the quality that is condemned by references to "the Jews" in narratives about things that took place in Judea is the self-righteous attitude among the religious leadership of the day. This is the very same religious zealotry that Jesus condemned many times,[209] and that serves as a stumbling block to overcome in the very first beatitude. That is why Paul preached:

> A man is not a Jew if he is only one outwardly, nor is circumcision merely outward and physical. No, a man is a Jew if he is one inwardly; and circumcision is circumcision of the heart, by the Spirit, not by the written code. Such a man's praise is not from men, but from God (Rom. 2:28–29).

It is significant that this observation was made by Paul, who by his own admission had been one of the most self-righteous persecutors of his day. And it serves as an admonition that if we are not truly "poor in spirit," if we are not truly aware that all of our righteous acts are no cleaner than "filthy rags," then we, too, can easily become persecutors, all while expecting—and even perceiving—persecution from unbelievers.[210]

---

207 Changing his name was a public profession of faith, for "Paul" is from the Latin "paululum," meaning "very small" or "very little." Thus, changing his name to Paul demonstrated that he was now "poor in spirit" and no longer relying on his own acts of righteousness.

208 Acts 9:4.

209 Indeed, it is the very same zealotry that we see in many Christians and Christian organizations today.

210 I am not suggesting that there is no persecution from the unbelieving world, but rather that the most insidious and dangerous persecution has always been and will always be from within the body of believers, from the false prophets and the tares among the wheat.

It is in this context that James Russell Lowell, the founding editor of the *Atlantic Monthly*,[211] penned his poem, "Once to Every Man and Nation."[212] In the poem, Lowell describes a choice between truth and falsehood that every generation faces. Those who choose truth are always persecuted, and by the time that the truth faced by a particular generation is universally accepted, another choice between truth and falsehood faces the next generation. Lowell was an abolitionist a full generation before the Civil War, yet he fully expected that one day slavery would be universally condemned as the evil that it is. He reached his conclusion by examining history, particularly the history of the church, and he described this phenomenon by declaring in the poem, "By the light of burning heretics Christ's bleeding feet I track."[213] The image painted by this line is that of a "heretic" being burned at the stake and the light from his pyre illuminating Christ's bloody feet. The point of the poem is that yesterday's "heretic" becomes tomorrow's martyr.

Thus, a maturing Christian will not merely accept as dogma that which he is told by the religious authorities of his day, but will instead satisfy his "hunger and thirst for righteousness" by diligent prayer and Bible study. In so doing, he will be communicating directly with God and will undoubtedly discern things about his faith that the religious authorities of the day have either ignored or denied. Ultimately, the maturing Christian will lovingly confront the errors he finds, and while other maturing Christians will respond in love, modern-day Pharisees will respond in anger. Thus, for the maturing Christian, *persecution is inevitable*.[214] Only after the passage of time will the persecuted "heretic" be dubbed a martyr, just as the Pharisees ultimately "revered" the prophets persecuted and slain by their ancestors:

> "Woe to you, teachers of the law and Pharisees, you hypocrites! You build tombs for the prophets and decorate the graves of the righteous. And you say, 'If we had lived in the days of our forefathers, we would not have taken part with them in shedding the blood of the prophets.' So you testify against yourselves that you are the descendants of those who murdered the prophets" (Matt. 23:29–31).

---

211 "Lowell, James Russell." James D. Hart, *The Concise Oxford Companion to American Literature*, Oxford, UK: Oxford University Press, 1986. *Oxford Reference Online*. Oxford University Press. Alabama Virtual Library. 3 August 2010 <http://www.oxfordreference.com/views/ENTRY.html?subview=Main&entry=t53.e1184>.

212 Paul Molloy, ed., *100 Plus American Poems*. New York: Scholastic Book Services, 1970. The poem is adapted from a longer work, *The Present Crisis*.

213 Ibid.

214 Second Corinthians 4:7–12; 2 Timothy 3:12–13; Hebrews 13:7; 1 Peter 3:12–14.

As if to prove this very point through irony, Lowell's poem was ultimately put to music and published as a hymn in the late nineteenth century, well after the Civil War had ended, but with a few subtle changes. One of those changes was to substitute for Lowell's word "heretics" the more easily swallowed word "martyrs."[215]

Like the Pharisees, we are fools when we think to ourselves, "If we had lived in the days of Jesus, we would not have shed His blood," and we are just as foolish when we fail to realize that many, many professing Christians believe just that. Those most susceptible to such thinking are those whose only exposure to God is a weekly spoon-feeding in church, for they obviously do not "hunger and thirst" for righteousness. It therefore follows that they may not even be "poor in spirit," for it is very difficult for souls "poor in spirit" to ignore their cravings for communion with God.

In addition, a spoon-fed Christian is not obeying Jesus, for Jesus did not command us to listen to the religious authorities.[216] Instead, He told us to obey what He taught and added that the Holy Spirit "will teach you all things and will remind you of everything I have said to you."[217] Thus, being led by the religious authorities rather than the Holy Spirit, the spoon-fed Christian is not likely to provoke persecution, and he is equally unlikely to ever distinguish the sheep from the wolves.

> "Watch out for false prophets. They come to you in sheep's clothing, but inwardly they are ferocious wolves. By their fruit you will recognize them. Do people pick grapes from thornbushes, or figs from thistles?" (Matt. 7:15).

But the maturing Christian, being led by the Holy Spirit and also being a diligent student of the Bible, will easily recognize the wolves and confront them. That is why the maturing Christian will ultimately be persecuted.

Fortunately, the Holy Spirit who leads the maturing Christian will also be there in his persecution, giving him the words to speak to his persecutors.[218] Indeed, persecution is not just evidence that a Christian is

---

215 I stumbled on this remarkable fact quite by chance. Already familiar with Lowell's poem, I happened to be looking at an old hymnal when I saw the "hymn." I had thought long and hard about Lowell's choice of words, especially the word "heretics," so the substitution of "martyrs" just jumped out at me.

216 I am not, of course, suggesting that no one listen to his minister or priest, or that we should avoid organized religious activity. But what I am saying is that the maturing Christian has the responsibility to feed himself spiritually and will ultimately be held accountable for this.

217 John 14:26.

218 Luke 12:11–12.

mature—it is evidence that he is led by the Holy Spirit. In his epistle to the Galatians, Paul makes this very point, calling maturing Christians led by the Holy Spirit "children of promise" and comparing them to Isaac.[219] He then reminds us that Isaac was persecuted by his half-brother, Ishmael, and concludes, "It is the same now."[220]

When we are persecuted, we must avoid an angry response, for Jesus taught us to respond in love: "Love your enemies and pray for those who persecute you."[221] Similarly, the apostle Paul taught, "Bless those who persecute you; bless and do not curse."[222] It is good, then, that the maturing Christian has the Holy Spirit on Whom to rely. Otherwise it would be impossible to obey Jesus, who commands us to rejoice in persecution.[223] But by willingly accepting persecution, we present ourselves as "living sacrifices" at God's altar[224] in obedience to Christ.

219 Galatians 4:28.

220 Galatians 4:29. Ishmael was born as the consequence of Abraham's lack of faith. Sarah, his wife, had urged him to sleep with her Egyptian maidservant, Hagar, because Sarah had been unable to conceive. Ishmael was the product of that union (Gen. 16:1–15). When God thereafter told Abraham that Sarah would conceive a son, he also made it clear that Sarah's son, Isaac, would be the heir to God's promises to Abraham (Gen. 17:1–22).

221 Matthew 5:44.

222 Romans 12:14.

223 Matthew 5:11–12; Luke 6:23.

224 Romans 12:1.

Questions for Further Study of the Eighth Beatitude

How is the fourth Beatitude related to the last? How is hunger and thirst for righteousness related to persecution? Is it possible to hunger and thirst for righteousness – to diligently read and study Scripture and continually pray to God – and not ultimately provoke persecution?

Have you ever been the subject of religious persecution? If so, was the source of the persecution religious or secular? If you have not been the subject of religious persecution, why do you suppose you have escaped it?

_____

_____

_____

_____

_____

_____

_____

_____

_____

_____

_____

_____

_____

_____

_____

_____

_____

_____

_____

_____

_____

_____

_____

_____

_____

_____

_____

_____

Blessed are Those Persecuted Because of Righteousness
by Robert Leslie Palmer

"Spare me!" we cry, seeking comfort from One
Who spared not Himself 'til victory He'd won.

Asking of God mere material gifts,
We miss divine bounty that changes and lifts.

Carnal our focus, and limited our sight,
We cling to our trinkets and see not the light.

Righteous we aren't, but righteous we'll be,
If we turn to our Lord and earnestly plea.

In place of our rags clean garments He gives,
And all of our sins He quickly forgives.

From that day forward we hunger and thirst,
Seeking God's blessings, with sacred the first.

In time we learn that the gifts that are best,
Are spiritual ones through which we are blessed.

Changing our hearts, God shows us the way,
To strengthen our souls for the imminent day.

Evil will find us then clinging to God,
Not to escape, but His footsteps to trod.

The Kingdom of Heaven

The subject of both the Beatitudes and the Sermon on the Mount is the kingdom of heaven. As stated above, I believe that the Beatitudes are simply Christ's introduction to his sermon, and that they concern the kingdom of heaven is supported by the fact that the kingdom of heaven is the promise in both the first and last beatitude. Significantly, Jesus also concludes the Sermon on the Mount with a reference to the kingdom of heaven:

> "Not everyone who says to me, 'Lord, Lord,' will enter the kingdom of heaven, but only he who does the will of my Father who is in heaven" (Matt. 7:21).

But just what does Jesus mean by "kingdom of heaven"? The Greek word translated as "kingdom" is βασιλεια ("basileia"),[225] which literally means "kingship," "royal rule," or "realm."[226] It did not originally incorporate the concept of a geographical "kingdom," but rather referred to the authority of the king.[227] The Greek word translated as "heaven" is ουρανος ("ouranos"),[228] which originally referred to the sky but came to refer to a physical place where God's throne is located and where Christians' rewards are stored.[229]

The phrase "kingdom of heaven" appears thirty-two times in thirty-one verses in the Bible, every time in Matthew. Mark, Luke, and John all

---

225 *Strong's*, G932; *Theology*, GK 993.
226 Ibid.
227 *Theology*, GK 993.
228 *Strong's*, G3772; *Theology*, GK 4041.
229 *Theology*, GK 4041. See Matthew 5:34–35; 6:20.

translated the phrase as "kingdom of God."[230] The phrase appears four times in the Sermon on the Mount, twice in the Beatitudes (in the first and last beatitudes), and twice more to warn the Pharisees that they would not inherit the kingdom.[231] Significantly, the phrase appears in eleven different parables,[232] all of which concern salvation, Christian growth, and Christian maturity. Those parables make several important points about the kingdom of heaven, including the following:

- First, the kingdom is worth more than any earthly treasure, and we should be willing to surrender all earthly treasure to gain the kingdom of heaven.

- Second, the kingdom is open to anyone who will accept salvation, but the time to act is now.

- Third, the law of love is the benchmark of the kingdom, and unless we are merciful to others (have compassion for them), we will not inherit the kingdom.[233]

- Fourth, after admission to the kingdom, we still have responsibilities, for we must use our talents to advance the kingdom.

- Fifth, until the Great White Throne Judgment, we will live and work among those serving Satan (the tares among the wheat), and in some cases, may not be able to tell the difference.

---

230 See, for example, Mark 4:26; Luke 6:20; John 3:3. Jesus spoke Aramaic, and the Gospel writers translated His teachings into Greek.

231 Matthew 5:20, 7:21. The point in these declarations is that the kingdom of heaven cannot be earned.

232 The parable of the weeds (Matt. 13:24–30; 36–43); the parable of the mustard seed (Matt. 13:31–32); the parable of the yeast (Matt. 13:33); the parable of the hidden treasure (Matt. 13:44); the parable of the valuable pearl (Matt. 13:45–46); the parable of the fish (Matt. 13:47–50); the parable of the unmerciful servant (Matt. 18:23–35); the parable of the workers in the field (Matt. 20:1–16); the parable of the wedding banquet (Matt. 22:2–14); the parable of the ten virgins (Matt. 25:1–13); and the parable of the talents (Matt. 25:14–30).

233 This does not mean that salvation can be lost, but rather that an unmerciful person has never truly accepted salvation and surrendered himself to God. Said another way, anyone who has truly accepted salvation has done so because he has acknowledged his own lack of righteousness, he has mourned his own spiritual death, and he has surrendered to God's will, and so his heart becomes merciful.

- Sixth, though its beginning is seemingly insignificant, the kingdom will eventually spread throughout the entire world.

But what is our role in the kingdom of heaven? As stated above in connection with the third beatitude, Jesus is the high priest[234] and the king of kings,[235] but we are to become priests[236] and kings[237] with him. That all Christians are to be kings in the kingdom of heaven is strange only if one thinks of an earthly kingdom, for the kingdom of heaven is not of this world,[238] and we are not called to be mere kings in the earthly sense but rather servant-kings.[239]

We should not forget that the kingdom is not something to be earned but is instead a free gift of God, given to those who trust Him. Indeed, as discussed in the overview above, the kingdom is a blessing. It is open to all who recognize that they have no righteousness apart from God[240] and so deserve death and hell,[241] and who therefore place their trust in Christ.[242]

---

234 Hebrews 2:17—3:1, 4:14, 5:1–10, 6:19–20.
235 First Timothy 6:15; Revelation 17:14, 19:16.
236 Revelation 1:6, 5:9–10, 20:6. See also Isaiah 61:6.
237 Second Timothy 2:12; Revelation 2:26–27, 3:21, 5:9–10.
238 John 18:36.
239 Luke 22:25–30.
240 That is, those who acknowledge that they are sinners. Isaiah 64:6; John 1:12–13; Romans 3:23; Romans 4:4; Ephesians 2:8–9.
241 Romans 6:23; Ezekiel 18:4.
242 John 3:16; John 3:36; Romans 3:22; Romans 10:9.

Archie's Journey

rchie represents the Christian "Everyteen," and his journey is intended to represent the Christian journey (see "Archie" in the glossary). For this reason, Archie's shield is a blue field with a white, eight-spoked wheel. This represents Archie's "invention" of the wheel, but more importantly, it represents the eight towers and his journey through the Beatitudes. The eight-spoked wheel was an early Christian symbol,[243] for it could be drawn by superimposing the capital Greek letters making up the word, "fish," IXΘΥΣ ("ichthus"),[244] one on top of another. The Greek letters spelling that word—iota, chi, theta, upsilon, and sigma—are an acrostic for the phrase, "Jesus Christ, God's son, savior," "Ιησους ('Iasus') Χριστος ('Christos'), Θεου ('theos') Υυιος ('huios'), Σοτηρ ('soter')," for they are the first letters of the Greek words making up that phrase.

The structure of the inscriptions of K'truum-Shra is similar to the structure of the Beatitudes, and Archie draws the same conclusions about them as I have drawn about the Beatitudes. First, just as the Beatitudes begin and end with the promise of the "kingdom of heaven," the inscriptions of K'truum-Shra begin and end with the promise of a "path to freedom." This, of course, is intended to equate home and freedom to heaven and the city of K'truum-Shra to our present life. Similarly, the structure of

---

243 http://www.plymouth-church.com/ichthus.html (August 3, 2010); http://symboldictionary.net/?p=2963 (August 3 2010); http://www.timelesswoodturnings.com/ichthus_page.html (August 3, 2010); http://en.wikipedia.org/wiki/Icthus (May 2, 2010).

244 The Greek letter sigma is most often written as "Σ," but was sometimes written as "C." Thus, the word "ichthys" would normally be written as "IXΘΥΣ," but in connection with the eight-spoked wheel symbol could be written as "IXΘΥC."

the city itself is intended to represent the manner in which the Beatitudes relate to each other.

Archie and the Tower of Humility

The first tower has the inscription, "Humility is the path to freedom" at its base. This represents the first beatitude, "Blessed are the poor in spirit, for theirs is the kingdom of heaven."[245] The things that happen to Archie at and around this tower therefore reflect the humility to which the first beatitude refers.

Initially, Archie becomes associated with the first tower and its lord, Pwrådisa, only after he declines knighthood. This, of course, is a form of humility, but not quite the humility to which the first beatitude refers. Then, at the very outset of his training, after sleeping in the rain, Archie and the other squire candidates are reduced to nothing, eating their meals naked while their clothes dry. Humility is much like that cold nakedness, for many of the perceptions we have about ourselves do nothing more than hide what is just below the surface. But perhaps more important, as discussed above in connection with the Beatitudes, righteousness is often symbolically associated in Scripture with garments, and so it is fitting that the boys are forced to eat their meals naked while their "filthy rags" are dried over the fire. They are symbolically ready to receive new garments of righteousness.

It is also at the first tower that Lord Pwrådisa gives Archie his dolphin and offers him a new suit of flexible armor. Lord Pwrådisa represents the Messiah both *before* death and resurrection and again *after* he is revealed to be the true king (see "Pwrådisa" in the glossary). The gift of a dolphin is intended to represent the free gift of salvation (see "Splasher" in the glossary) and the flexible armor is intended to represent the fact that God equips us for spiritual warfare (see "Armor" in the glossary).

Although the Tower of Humility is the first tower, throughout the novel Archie returns to that tower, for the kind of humility to which the first beatitude refers is essential to development of every other character trait that is the subject of any of the Beatitudes. For example, the secret underwater passageway between the Tower of Humility and the Tower of Compassion exemplifies the relationship between the first and fifth beatitudes. The old bearded knight summarizes this by saying that "compassion always flows

---

245 Matthew 5:3.

from humility." In short, one must be truly "poor in spirit" to show the kind of compassion about which the fifth beatitude speaks.

Finally, Archie's journey through the underwater passageway between the Tower of Humility and the Tower of Compassion represents the transition between the first four beatitudes, which concern the attitudes and actions involved in *becoming* a Christian, and the last four beatitudes, which concern the *maturing* Christian. Thus, in the passageway Archie is forced to swim underwater in faith, which itself is symbolic of believer's baptism.

Archie and the Tower of Mourning

The second tower has the inscription, "Mourning leads to change" at its base. This represents the second beatitude, "Blessed are those who mourn, for they will be comforted."[246] The things that happen to Archie at and around this tower therefore reflect the spiritual mourning to which the second beatitude refers. It is only after he is imprisoned in the second tower that Archie finally understands that he is a sinner, and he reaches this conclusion only with the help of T'lôt'aris, the old bearded knight. T'lôt'aris is a knight in service to Lord Pwrâdisa. He represents the Holy Spirit, and he uses the Socratic method of instruction, asking questions to lead his student to find the answers himself and to learn how to think critically (see "T'lôt'aris" in the glossary).

During his imprisonment, Archie first blames everyone but himself for his predicament. But with the help of the old bearded knight, he comes to realize that it is his own fault that he is in the dungeon. As soon as he acknowledges that fact, the old bearded knight informs Archie that Lord Pwrâdisa is willing to represent him as his counsel at his trial, and Archie accepts the offer.

After his trial and Lord Pwrâdisa's sacrifice, Archie meets N'derlex at the Tower of Mourning, where the Alliance headquarters are located. N'derlex represents the *risen* Messiah (see "N'derlex" in the glossary). He is the military leader of the Alliance and the lawful heir and Lord of the house associated with the Tower of Sacrifice, which is also associated with the throne. That Christ is represented by two people in the novel is not intended to suggest that there is more than one savior, but rather to symbolize Archie's relationship with that single savior before and after accepting salvation.

---

246 Matthew 5:4.

The secret underwater passageway between the Tower of Mourning and the Tower of Purity symbolizes that unless one mourns one's own sins, he cannot ever hope to be pure in heart and that even believers must continue to have a repentant heart if they want to see with holy vision. Thus, after Archie is captured by Thlū'taku, who represents Satan (see "Thlū'taku" in the glossary), he must escape by taking that secret underwater passageway back to the Tower of Mourning. It is no accident that this occurs after Archie is tempted by Thlū'taku and actually sees Thlū'taku's face in his own reflection.

Archie and the Tower of Surrender

The third tower has the inscription "Surrender is gain" at its base. This represents the third beatitude, "Blessed are the meek, for they will inherit the earth."[247] The things that happen to Archie at and around this tower therefore reflect the meekness to which the third beatitude refers.

Although Archie has symbolically accepted salvation at the second tower, it is at the third tower that he learns that he must obey and surrender his will. Archie meets the old bearded knight as he is running near the Tower of Surrender, and the old bearded knight then leads him to the library where he must study the ancient scrolls, which, of course, represent Scripture. It is also at the Tower of Surrender that Archie is knighted, which symbolically represents the transformation that has taken place in his life.

The secret underwater passageway between the Tower of Surrender and the Tower of Peace symbolizes the relationship between the third and seventh beatitudes. This is summarized when the old bearded knight tells Archie "You will always have conflict, but to have peace in spite of conflict, you must learn to *trust*. And to trust, you must become *obedient*. You must therefore surrender your will and accept your circumstances, whatever they may be. When you can do that, peace will reign in your heart."

Archie and the Tower of Morality

The fourth tower has the inscription, "Morality is possible only when it is impossible." This represents the fourth beatitude, "Blessed are those who hunger and thirst for righteousness, for they will be filled."[248] The

---

247 Matthew 5:5.
248 Matthew 5:6.

things that happen to Archie at and around this tower therefore reflect the righteousness to which the fourth beatitude refers.

Archie's first experience associated with the Tower of Morality is his encounter with the refugees after his first battle. It was at that tower that he sought forgiveness for the refugees, proclaiming, "But these people were deceived by Thlū'taku and have realized that following him was wrong—shouldn't we now forgive them?" When the old bearded knight did not respond, Archie secretly swelled with pride, thinking that for once the last word was his. Later, when Archie found Mo'kea after the second battle, the old bearded knight asked, "Just a few short hours ago a young knight said to me, 'These people were deceived by Thlū'taku and have realized that following him was wrong—shouldn't we now forgive them?' Do you recall from whose lips I heard those words, Sleeper?" The purpose of these events is to demonstrate that morality is, in fact, impossible when we rely on our own virtue, for it is easy to "forgive" strangers who have not wronged us, but it is quite another thing to forgive those who have hurt us.

Later, in the fig orchard associated with the Tower of Morality, the old bearded knight leads Archie to conclude that he is incapable of morality, then surprises him by saying, "Then, Sleeper, I submit that you *are* capable of morality, for you *know* that you are not good and that you are not capable of morality on your own. For so long as you bear that in mind, you are capable of morality, for that is what the inscription means."

It is no accident that the fig orchard is associated in the novel with the Tower of Morality, for the fig is a symbol of faith and the fruits of faith[249] (see "Fig" in the glossary). The righteousness about which the fourth beatitude speaks is the righteousness with which God cloaks us when we have faith.

The secret underwater passageway between the Tower of Morality and the Tower of Sacrifice symbolizes the relationship between the fourth and eighth beatitudes. As explained in the discussion of the beatitudes above, the first four beatitudes all concern a change in the heart associated with becoming a believer, and the next four beatitudes concern Christian maturity. Thus, it is only logical that the first four beatitudes are mirrored in the final four, and this is symbolized by the secret underwater passageways. It is in this context that morality leads to sacrifice and that true righteousness leads to persecution.

---

249 Matthew 24:32; Luke 13:6–9.

Archie and the Tower of Compassion

The Fifth Tower, the Tower of Compassion, has the inscription "Compassion begets compassion" at its base. This represents the fifth beatitude, "Blessed are the merciful, for they will be shown mercy."[250] The things that happen to Archie at and around this tower therefore reflect the active compassion to which the fifth beatitude refers.

It is at the Tower of Compassion that Archie seeks Lord Mókato, for he had promised Mo'kea that he would try to save her grandfather. Instead, he learns that Lord Mókato is dead and then he is confronted with forgiving Kótan. Archie had mentally prepared himself to forgive Lord Mókato, but he had not given any thought to Kótan. This is intended to suggest that God does not want us to forgive out of our own power or because we are prepared to do so, but instead to rely on Him in forgiving those who have wronged us. Archie must struggle with this, but is helped by the fact that Kótan is a broken man. Indeed, Kótan clearly expresses this fact when he proclaims, "I am nothing and always was. Why should I care who wins this war or what my fate shall be? It is all *meaningless*." In saying this, Kótan echoes King Solomon, who declared in Ecclesiastes, "'Meaningless! Meaningless!' says the Teacher. 'Utterly meaningless! Everything is meaningless.'"[251]

His heart stirred to compassion, Archie tells Kótan, "Your life is not meaningless, and you are not dead yet." This shows that Archie understands that Kótan is ready for salvation, and it is the logical response, for Archie too has echoed Ecclesiastes, at the conclusion of which King Solomon declared, "Remember your Creator … before the silver cord is severed, or the golden bowl is broken; before the pitcher is shattered at the spring, or the wheel broken at the well, and the dust returns to the ground it came from, and the spirit returns to God who gave it."[252]

It is significant in the story that Archie arrives at the Tower of Compassion only after working his way through the secret underwater passageway from the Tower of Humility. Thus, the old bearded knight, having witnessed Archie forgiving Kótan, declared, "You have twice made the passage from humility to compassion." Later, after making Archie realize the futility and danger of pride, he explains, "The first passage was from tower to tower, the second from heart to heart … just as surely as anger and hatred are fruits of pride, compassion *always* flows from humility."

---

250 Matthew 5:7.
251 Ecclesiastes 1:2.
252 Ecclesiastes 12:1–7.

Archie and the Tower of Purity

The sixth tower has at its base the inscription, "Purity restores the blind." This represents the sixth beatitude, "Blessed are the pure in heart, for they will see God."[253] The things that happen to Archie at and around this tower therefore reflect the purity to which the sixth beatitude refers.

Archie's first significant experience at the Tower of Purity is the startling conclusion of chapter 18, in which he sees Thlū'taku's face in his own reflection. On other occasions in the same tower, he sees Thlū'taku's face in the brassy and bellicose knight's countenance and Lord Pwrâdisa's face in N'derlex. Thus, the tower symbolizes the fact that believers who are pure in heart will not only see God, but also see others as God sees them.

Thlū'taku represents Satan (see "Thlū'taku" in the glossary). It is therefore significant that Archie saw Thlū'taku's face in his own reflection when he was contemplating Thlū'taku's offer, and this suggests that God will give us the vision not only to differentiate between the wheat and the tares, but also to recognize when we are being tempted. It is for the same reason that Archie sees Thlū'taku's face in the brassy and bellicose knight's countenance.

But Thlū'taku is not the only face Archie sees at the Tower of Purity, for it is there that he sees Lord Pwrâdisa's face in N'derlex. Significantly, this occurs only after Archie pledges his complete obedience to N'derlex, thereby suggesting once again the connection between the second and sixth beatitudes. Our hearts are purest when we not only recognize that we are sinful but are also repentant and obedient.

It is also at the Tower of Purity that Archie discovers that T'lôt'aris and N'derlex are not as far away as he thought. In chapter 18, when Archie realized that the permanent Alliance headquarters were located at the other end of the city, he concluded in despair that, "Even if they wanted to, N'derlex and T'lotaris could not rescue him." But when he learned of the plan to rescue him, and that it involved a secret underwater passageway between the Tower of Purity and the Tower of Mourning, Archie realized that "his fear that N'derlex and T'lôt'aris were so far away and could never reach him was clearly very wrong." God, too, has promised us that He is never far away and will not forsake us.[254] Understanding this with our hearts as well as our minds is another way of "seeing" God.

Toward the end of the novel, Archie begins to see Thlū'taku's face more consistently in the supporters of the brassy and bellicose knight, even when he is not near the Tower of Purity. This is intended to symbolize the increasing acuity of "holy" vision in the more fully matured believer.

253 Matthew 5:8.
254 Hebrews 13:5.

Archie and the Tower of Peace

The seventh tower has the inscription "Peace is the mark of true royalty" at its base. This represents the seventh beatitude, "Blessed are the peacemakers, for they will be called sons of God."[255] The things that happen to Archie at and around this tower therefore reflect the peace to which the seventh beatitude refers.

The Tower of Peace is one of the last two towers captured by the Alliance, so it can be said that the war ends at the Tower of Peace. But this is not the peace that is most significant in the story. Instead, the peace that is most important is the peace within Archie's heart, a peace that comes from surrender and obedience. Thus, Archie's last resistance is overcome during his conversation with the old bearded knight in the olive grove associated with the Tower of Peace. There Archie learned about how olives grow better when grafted onto an older tree with more established roots, and that to have peace he would have to be obedient to the king, trusting him wholeheartedly. This is summarized when the old bearded knight tells Archie "You will always have conflict, but to have peace in spite of conflict, you must learn to *trust*. And to trust, you must become *obedient*. You must therefore surrender your will and accept your circumstances, whatever they may be. When you can do that, peace will reign in your heart." Archie demonstrated this faithful obedience as he made his way through the secret underwater passageway back to the Tower of Surrender, where he made up his mind to pledge his fealty to N'derlex.

Archie and the Tower of Sacrifice

The eighth tower has the inscription "Sacrifice is the path to freedom" at its base. This represents the eighth beatitude, "Blessed are those who are persecuted because of righteousness, for theirs is the kingdom of heaven."[256] The things that happen to Archie at and around this tower therefore reflect the persecution to which the eighth beatitude refers.

As stated above, the eighth beatitude concerns the world's reaction to a maturing Christian rather than an internal attribute of the Christian. This is highlighted in the novel by the fact that Archie cannot find either T'lôt'aris or N'derlex after the conclusion of the war. He is therefore left alone in the vineyard trying to discover the meaning of the eighth inscription.

---

255 Matthew 5:9.
256 Matthew 5:10.

This does not mean that Archie has been abandoned, for Archie does finally hear the old bearded knight's voice when he is brought before the counterfeit king. As stated above in the discussion of the Beatitudes, we have been promised that in our persecution, the Holy Spirit will guide us and give us the words to speak to our persecutors.[257] But we have not been promised that we will know in advance the form in which persecution will come, and we should thank God for this blessing. I, for one, would certainly hate to have the specifics penciled in on my calendar, and if they were, I would be tempted to call in sick when the day of persecution arrived.

Archie is flogged, mocked, and sentenced to death, just as Jesus was. But instead of crucifixion, he and the other believers are sentenced to be devoured by sharks. Aside from being appropriate for a city floating in the ocean, the purpose is to symbolize the fact that all our persecutors can take from us is flesh, not spirit. And Archie's prolonged torture is intended to fit the conclusion of the story, for he loses consciousness as he is drowning, but then awakens to learn that he was saved from drowning.[258]

Just as the fully mature believer receives the kingdom of heaven after enduring persecution, Archie finds the "path to freedom," which, for him, is the way home.

---

257 Luke 12:11–12.
258 Matthew 16:25.

Glossary
Characters and Symbols

Apple: Associated in the novel with the Tower of Compassion, the apple is symbolic of both love and the original sin.[259] Thus, it is also an appropriate symbol for the Tower of Compassion because, as T'lôt'aris tells Archie, "Compassion *always* flows from humility." True biblical love and compassion are possible only when we do not fail to remember that we, too, are sinners.

Archie: Introduced in chapter 1, Archie represents the Christian "Everyteen." His given name, "Archibald," is a Germanic name meaning "genuine" and "bold,"[260] thereby reminding us that our hope in Christ should make us bold.[261] His surname, "Zwick," is an obscure surname, also of Germanic origin, meaning "triangle" or "wedge," particularly in reference to one who farmed a triangular-shaped piece of land.[262] It is intended to evoke images of the Bermuda triangle, where Archie was lost at sea, as well as the eight triangular wedges forming the city of K'truum-Shra. More important, however, the surname is a hint that he is on a divine journey, for it is suggestive of the Holy Trinity. Indeed, Archie's initials are the first and last letters of the alphabet, which is intended to call to mind that he is symbolically seeking God, the Alpha and Omega. This is also why his surname is mentioned only in the first and last chapters

259 Jack Tresidder, *The Complete Dictionary of Symbols*. San Francisco, CA: Chronicle Books, 2004.

260 Hanks, Patrick & Hodges, Flavia, *A Dictionary of First Names*. New York: Oxford University Press, 1990.

261 Second Corinthians 3:12.

262 Elsdon C. Smith, *American Surnames*, Baltimore, MD: Genealogical Publishing Company, Inc., 1994.

of the novel. He is known as "Archie" to everyone but T'lôt'aris, who calls him "Sleeper," a nickname with two purposes. First, it is intended to foreshadow the conclusion of the story, in which Archie awakens out of a deep sleep. Second, it is also intended to suggest the sleep-like state in which Christians now live, for, "Now we see but a poor reflection as in a mirror; then we shall see face to face. Now I know in part; then I shall know fully, even as I am fully known."[263] Archie's shield is a blue field with a white, eight-spoked wheel. This represents Archie's "invention" of the wheel, but more importantly, it represents the eight towers and his journey through the Beatitudes (see "Wheel" below).

Armor: The flexible armor that Lord Pwrådisa gives to Archie is a gift to replace the musky old armor with which he trained. This represents the fact that God equips us to fight the spiritual battles we encounter. "Therefore put on the full armor of God, so that when the day of evil comes, you may be able to stand your ground, and after you have done everything, to stand."[264]

Be'lak: Captain Be'lak is the Alliance spy who rescues Archie when he is held captive by Thlŭ'taku, and he later joins his forces with Archie's forces to help defeat Thlŭ'taku in a major offensive. Although he is introduced in chapter 18, Archie does not learn Be'lak's name until chapter 23. His name is derived from "Caleb," one of the twelve spies sent by Moses to the Promised Land.[265] Only two of those spies were unafraid of what they saw, for they placed their faith in God rather than in their own strength. Caleb demonstrated that faith when he silenced the rebellious Israelites. "Then Caleb silenced the people before Moses and said, 'We should go up and take possession of the land, for we can certainly do it.'"[266] Because he was loyal to God, he survived the years of wandering in the wilderness and was given Hebron as his portion in the Promised Land. Again demonstrating his trust in God, Caleb eagerly set about conquering Hebron even though by that time he was eighty-five years old.[267] Captain Be'lak therefore represents the unconquerable spirit that God will give us if we trust Him.

---

263 First Corinthians 13:12. See also John 11:11–15.
264 Ephesians 6:13.
265 Numbers 13:1–25.
266 Numbers 13:30.
267 Joshua 14:1–15.

Blue and White: Unlike the other shields in the story, those of N'derlex, T'lôt'aris, and Archie all have blue fields with simple white symbols. Blue is a heraldic symbol of eternity, truth, devotion, faith, purity, fidelity, steadfastness, and spiritual life.[268] White is a symbol of purity, truth, wisdom, innocence, cleanliness, peace, sincerity, joy, and the sacred or divine.[269] It is appropriate for N'derlex and T'lôt'aris to bear these colors because they represent the divine. It is appropriate for Archie to bear these colors because he is on a divine journey.

Citron: Associated in the novel with the Tower of Surrender, the citron is a symbol of submission to God's will. In the Bible, it is referred to as the "choice fruit,"[270] and it is one of the "four species"[271] used in the liturgy of Sukkot.[272] Because the citron is heart shaped, it symbolizes the heart,[273] the place of understanding and wisdom. During the ceremony, the branches of the other three species are bound together and held in the right hand and waved over the citron, which is held in the left hand, closest to the heart.[274] The ritual waving symbolizes the sovereignty of God.[275] Thus, the citron is an apt symbol of the submission of the heart to God's sovereignty.

Date Palm: Associated in the novel with the Tower of Mourning, the date palm is rich with symbolism in all its elements. The palm branch is a

---

268 Jack Tresidder, *The Complete Dictionary of Symbols.* San Francisco: Chronicle Books, 2004; Ottfried Neubecker, *A Guide to Heraldry*, New York: Barnes & Noble, 2007.

269 Ibid.

270 Leviticus 23:40.

271 Michael Strassfeld, *The Jewish Holidays: A Guide & Commentary.* New York: Harper & Row, 1985; "Etrog." John Bowker, ed., *The Concise Oxford Dictionary of World Religions*, Oxford, UK: Oxford University Press, 2000. *Oxford Reference Online.* Oxford University Press. Alabama Virtual Library. 3 August 2010. <http://www.oxfordreference.com/views/ENTRY.html?subview=Main&entry=t101.e2311>.

272 The Feast of Tabernacles. "Sukkot" is plural. The singular is "sukkah."

273 "Symbolism." Louis Jacobs, *A Concise Companion to the Jewish Religion.* Oxford, UK: Oxford University Press, 1999. *Oxford Reference Online.* Oxford University Press. Alabama Virtual Library. 3 August 2010 <http://www.oxfordreference.com/views/ENTRY.html?subview=Main&entry=t96.e670>.

274 "Four Species." John Bowker, ed., *The Concise Oxford Dictionary of World Religions*. Oxford, UK: Oxford University Press, 2000. *Oxford Reference Online.* Oxford University Press. Alabama Virtual Library. 3 August 2010. <http://www.oxfordreference.com/views/ENTRY.html?subview=Main&entry=t101.e2518>.

275 "Tabernacles." Louis Jacobs, *A Concise Companion to the Jewish Religion*, Oxford, UK: Oxford University Press, 1999. *Oxford Reference Online.* Oxford University Press. Alabama Virtual Library. 3 August 2010. <http://www.oxfordreference.com/views/ENTRY.html?subview=Main&entry=t96.e681>

symbol of victory and resurrection[276] because palm branches were strewn before Jesus as He entered Jerusalem on Palm Sunday.[277] It is also a symbol of spiritual reflection, mourning, and repentance, for the ashes used to mark a cross on the foreheads of Christians during Lent are traditionally from burned palm fronds.[278] But even before Christ, the date palm was already a biblical symbol. Deborah, the prophetess and judge, held court under a date palm when she led Israel.[279] The date itself is a symbol of the just,[280] and the righteous are compared to a palm tree.[281] Like the pomegranate, the date palm is associated with both the Temple[282] and the Messiah.[283]

Dolphaeton: The dolphaeton is a fictional water carriage resembling a phaeton, a sporty open carriage drawn by a single horse or a pair with four large wheels and a minimal body.[284] The phaeton's name is an allusion to the mythical Phaëton (also spelled "Phaethon"),[285] who persuaded his father, Helios, the Greek sun god, to let him drive his sun chariot one day.[286] Because he was unable to control the chariot, he set the earth ablaze, so Zeus destroyed him with a thunderbolt, and he fell from the sky like a falling star.[287] The prophet Isaiah referred to Satan as a fallen star,[288] and some believe that this is an allusion to Phaëton.[289] Thus, the dolphaeton is intended to foreshadow the imminent war in which Thlũ'taku is defeated.

276 Jack Tresidder, *The Complete Dictionary of Symbols*. San Francisco, CA: Chronicle Books, 2004.

277 John 12:12–13.

278 Sarah Goodfellow, Sheila Jennett, "forehead," *The Oxford Companion to the Body*. Edited by Colin Blakemore and Sheila Jennett. Oxford, UK: Oxford University Press, 2001. *Oxford Reference Online*. Oxford University Press. Alabama Virtual Library. 3 August 2010 <http://www.oxfordreference.com/views/ENTRY.html?subview=Main&entry=t128.e387>.

279 Judges 4:4–5.

280 Jack Tresidder, *The Complete Dictionary of Symbols*. San Francisco, CA: Chronicle Books, 2004.

281 Psalm 92:12.

282 First Kings 6:29.

283 John 12:13; Revelation 7:9.

284 "Phaeton." Morton S. Freeman, *A New Dictionary of Eponyms*, Oxford, UK: Oxford University Press, 1997. *Oxford Reference Online*. Oxford University Press. Alabama Virtual Library. 3 August 2010 <http://www.oxfordreference.com/views/ENTRY.html?subview=Main&entry=t31.e288>.

285 Ibid.

286 Guus Houtzager, *The Complete Encyclopedia of Greek Mythology: The World of the Greek Gods and Heroes in Words and Pictures*. Edison, NJ: Chartwell Books, 2003. Edith Hamilton, *Mythology*. New York: Little Brown & Co., 1942.

287 Ibid.

288 Isaiah 14:12.

289 "Lucifer" JewishEncyclopedia.com. 3 August 2010 <http://www.jewishencyclopedia.com/view.jsp?artid=612&letter=L&search=lucifer>.

That it belongs to Lord Mókato and his granddaughter, Mókea, points to their involvement with Thlū'taku.

Fig: Associated in the novel with the Tower of Morality, the fig is a symbol of faith and the fruits of faith.[290] The fig is also one of the seven types of fruits and grains enumerated in the Old Testament as being special products of the land of Israel.[291]

Freedom: Just as the first and last of the Beatitudes both promise the "kingdom of heaven," the first and last of the eight inscriptions on the towers both refer to the "path to freedom." Archie figures out that for him, freedom refers to his home (see "Home" below). The floating city of K'truum-Shra represents the Beatitudes collectively (see "K'truum-Shra" below). And as explained in the discussion of the Beatitudes above, I believe that the Beatitudes introduce and summarize the Sermon on the Mount and indeed, Christ's teachings. Jesus told us, "If you hold to my teaching, you are really my disciples. Then you will know the truth, and the truth will set you free."[292]

Glutton: K'lud'pe, dubbed "Glutton" by the old bearded knight, is introduced in chapter 7, along with Liar, Sloth, and Whiner. He represents those who receive the word but choose instead to pursue the desires of flesh. "The one who received the seed that fell among the thorns is the man who hears the word, but ... the deceitfulness of wealth choke it, making it unfruitful."[293]

Grapes: Associated in the novel with the Tower of Sacrifice, the vine is a heraldic symbol of eternal life[294] and a scriptural symbol of both Christ's sacrifice and the kingdom of heaven.[295] The vine is also one of the seven types of fruits and grains enumerated in the Old Testament as being special products of the land of Israel.[296]

Home: Throughout the novel, Archie deeply desires to return to his home, and this longing for home symbolizes Christian longing for heaven. "But

---

290 Matthew 24:32; Luke 13:6–9.
291 Deuteronomy 8:7–9.
292 John 8:31–32.
293 Matthew 13:22.
294 Jack Tresidder, *The Complete Dictionary of Symbols.* San Francisco, CA: Chronicle Books, 2004.
295 Luke 22:20; Matthew 20:1–16.
296 Deuteronomy 8:7–9.

in keeping with his promise we are looking forward to a new heaven and a new earth, the home of righteousness."[297] Indeed, as Christians, we are to view our lives on this earth as transitory and regard ourselves as ambassadors of heaven.[298]

K'truum: K'truum is a mysterious substance that is harder than steel yet light enough to float. Apart from the "k" added in front (to make the name more mysterious), the name is intended to evoke an image of "steel." Thus, it has two blended consonants followed by a double vowel and then a single consonant. By virtue of being solid, lightweight, and glowing, k'truum represents the nature of Christ's teachings. Those teachings are solid enough to be like the rock upon which the wise man builds his house[299] and yet not a heavy burden.[300] They are also a light to the world.[301] It is only fitting that a city that itself represents the Beatitudes—a summary of Christ's teachings—should be constructed of a substance with all of these qualities.

K'truum-Shra: K'truum-Shra, the floating city that is the primary setting for the novel, represents the Beatitudes collectively. The choice of three syllables is deliberate and is intended to evoke images of other mysterious places, both fictional and real, such as Shangri-la, Angkor-wat, Xanadu, Valhala, Shambhala, and Atlantis.

Kótan: Kótan, the premier k'truum-smith in the city, is introduced in chapter 9. He represents fellow sinners ready for harvest whom we meet on our Christian journeys. His name is derived from Vulcan, the Roman god of fire and metalworking who manufactured arms and armor for various gods and heroes.[302] His name also sounds very much like "Cotton," the surname of the fisherman resembling Kótan who rescued Archie. That Mr. Cotton is a fisherman and fished Archie out of the water, thereby saving him, reminds us that we are to be "fishers of men."[303] It also echoes Kótan's final heroic act in saving many of the crew of the doomed "submarine."

---

297 Second Peter 3:13.
298 Second Corinthians 5:20; Ephesians 6:20.
299 Matthew 7:24.
300 Matthew 11:30.
301 Matthew 4:16.
302 Guus Houtzager, *The Complete Encyclopedia of Greek Mythology: The World of the Greek Gods and Heroes in Words and Pictures.* Edison, NJ. Chartwell Books, 2003. Edith Hamilton, *Mythology.* New York: Little Brown & Co., 1942. Vulcan is the equivalent of the Greek god Hephaestus or Hephaestos.
303 Matthew 4:19; Mark 1:17.

Liar: N'joph'n, dubbed "Liar" by the old bearded knight, is introduced in chapter 7, along with Glutton, Sloth, and Whiner. He represents those who receive the word but do not understand it. "When anyone hears the message about the kingdom and does not understand it, the evil one comes and snatches away what was sown in his heart. This is the seed sown along the path."[304]

L'teif: First Sergeant L'teif, introduced in chapter 14, represents the steadfast Christian friend. His name is derived from the word "fidelity."

Mókato: Lord Mókato, introduced in chapter 2, represents the Old Testament law. He is the 613th Elder of Elders, the leader of the city of K'truum-Shra. This is intended to represent the 613 commandments in the Old Testament.[305] He is also the grandfather of Mókea and the Lord of the House associated with the Tower of Purity. Because he represents the Old Testament law, the purity he symbolizes is a false purity, the false purity assumed by the Pharisees.[306] The traditional shields associated with each of the eight towers had a gold field with a black chief (thick bar at top), a black border, and a black inescutcheon (internal shield) with a single white tower. They differed only in the three items in the chief, depictions in white of the fruit, fish, and grain associated with the individual tower. But Lord Mókato's shield had been altered in two ways. First, a gold crown was added over the white tower in the inescutcheon. This was a permissible change to signify that he was the current Elder of Elders. Second, the fruit, fish, and grain in the chief had been replaced by six smaller white towers, representing the six towers that no longer had any lords. This was an impermissible change.

Mókea: Mókea, introduced in chapter 2, represents temptation, and she is therefore exceptionally beautiful. Although she has the same general appearance as the other T'lantim, her eyes are a brilliant green and sometimes appear to glow in the dark. She is the granddaughter of Lord Mókato, suggesting that the Old Testament law, by being impossible to fulfill, gives birth to temptation, which in turn leads us to repentance. "So the law was put in charge to lead us to Christ that we might be justified

---

304 Matthew 13:19.

305 "Six hundred and thirteen commandments." John Bowker, ed., *The Concise Oxford Dictionary of World Religions*, Oxford, UK: Oxford University Press, 2000. *Oxford Reference Online.* Oxford University Press. Alabama Virtual Library. 3 August 2010 <http://www.oxfordreference.com/views/ENTRY.html?subview=Main&entry=t101.e6848>.

306 Matthew 23:25–28.

by faith."[307] Mókea is also betrothed to Thlŭ'taku, thereby suggesting that temptation is the bride of Satan. She initially tempts Archie to disobey the law, so that he will be cut off from his master, Lord Pwrâdisa. After Archie repents and is restored, she tempts him to "pay" for his wrongdoing, thereby trying to make him focus on works rather than faith. Mókea is therefore symbolic of both the world's temptation of the unbeliever and the temptation of believers by the tares and false prophets within the church. That she is the first to greet Archie as he emerges from the bedroom in which he first found himself suggests that temptation greets us as we emerge from the womb.

N'derlex: N'derlex, introduced in chapter 13, represents the *risen* Messiah. He is the military leader of the Alliance and the lawful heir and Lord of the house associated with the Tower of Sacrifice, which is also associated with the throne. His name is derived from the name "Alexander" in order to evoke images of Alexander the Great. His shield has a blue field with a white anchor. The anchor is a symbol of Christian salvation, and in early Christian burial carvings, an anchor is often depicted flanked by a dolphin,[308] a symbol of salvation (see Splasher below). The anchor is also a heraldic symbol of hope and Christian steadfastness.[309]

Neroh-Brougham: The neroh-brougham is a water-borne version of a brougham, a light, enclosed four-wheeled horse-drawn carriage named for Scottish jurist Henry Brougham,[310] First Baron Brougham and Vaux, Lord Chancellor of Great Britain.[311] "The Lord Chancellor is the presiding officer of the House of Lords and the head of the judiciary in the United Kingdom."[312] Thus, the fact that the neroh-brougham belongs to Lord

---

307 Galatians 3:24.
308 Hans Biedermann, *Dictionary of Symbolism: Cultural Icons and the Meanings Behind Them*. Translated by James Hulbert. New York: Facts on File, 1992.
309 Ibid.
310 "Brougham." T. F. Hoad, ed., *The Concise Oxford Dictionary of English Etymology*. Oxford, UK: Oxford University Press, 1996. *Oxford Reference Online*. Oxford University Press. Alabama Virtual Library. 3 August 2010 <http://www.oxfordreference.com/views/ENTRY.html?subview=Main&entry=t27.e1888>.
311 "Brougham, Henry Peter, 1st Baron Brougham and Vaux." John Cannon, ed., *A Dictionary of British History*. Oxford, UK: Oxford University Press, 2009. *Oxford Reference Online*. Oxford University Press. Alabama Virtual Library. 3 August 2010 <http://www.oxfordreference.com/views/ENTRY.html?subview=Main&entry=t43.e533>.
312 "Lord Chancellor *noun*." Catherine Soanes and Angus Stevenson, ed., *The Oxford Dictionary of English* (revised edition), Oxford, UK: Oxford University Press, 2005. *Oxford Reference Online*. Oxford University Press. Alabama Virtual Library. 3 August 2010 <http://www.oxfordreference.com/views/ENTRY.html?subview=Main&entry=t140.e44914>.

Pwrâdisa hints at his true position both as the king (presiding over all other lords) and as judge.

Olive: Associated in the novel with the Tower of Peace, the olive is a scriptural symbol of peace, particularly between God and man.[313] Israel was not the only ancient nation to associate the olive with peace. Roman messengers seeking peace carried olive branches wrapped in wool.[314] But the olive is symbolic of much more, for the oil made from olives was very important in the ancient world. Olive oil was prized for its ability to soften, cleanse, and treat wounds, as well as its use for food and fuel.[315] The olive also symbolizes the source of life, Jesus,[316] for the olive tree is an evergreen,[317] and it is one of the seven types of fruits and grains enumerated in the Old Testament as being special products of the land of Israel.[318]

Orange: Associated in the novel with the Tower of Purity, the orange is itself a symbol of purity.[319]

Pomegranate: Associated in the novel with the Tower of Humility, the pomegranate is a symbol of resurrection and the sweetness of the heavenly kingdom.[320] It is a scriptural symbol of God's bountiful love, and its red juice symbolizes martyrdom.[321] The pomegranate is one of the seven types of fruits and grains enumerated in the Old Testament as being special products of the land of Israel,[322] and it is associated with both priests and the Temple.[323]

Pwrâdisa: Lord Pwrâdisa, introduced in chapter 5, represents the Messiah both *before* death and resurrection and again *after* he is revealed to be the true king. He is the Lord of the house associated with the Tower of

---

313 Genesis 8:11.
314 Hans Biedermann, *Dictionary of Symbolism: Cultural Icons and the Meanings Behind Them.* Translated by James Hulbert. New York: Facts on File, 1992.
315 Ibid.
316 Romans 11:17.
317 "Olive." Merrill C. Tenney, ed., *The Zondervan Pictorial Bible Dictionary*, Grand Rapids, MI: Zondervan, 1967.
318 Deuteronomy 8:7–9.
319 Jack Tresidder, *The Complete Dictionary of Symbols.* San Francisco, CA: Chronicle Books, 2004.
320 Ibid.
321 Hans Biedermann, *Dictionary of Symbolism: Cultural Icons and the Meanings Behind Them.* Translated by James Hulbert. New York: Facts on File, 1992.
322 Deuteronomy 8:7–9.
323 Exodus 28:33; 1 Kings 7:18; 2 Chronicles 3:16.

Humility, which is also associated with priests. His name is derived from "paradise," and his shield is the traditional shield of the lords of the eight towers (see Mókato above), depicting the fruit, fish, and grain associated with his house (pomegranate, tuna, and corn). At the jousting match with Thlū'taku, he is unseated on the third pass, which is intended to symbolize that Christ rose on the third day. His unseating may not seem to be an apt symbol of resurrection, but it is later revealed that he deliberately allowed himself to be unseated in order to save Archie.

Sacred Necklace: Introduced in chapter 3, the sacred necklace represents the fact that God promised to write His commands directly onto our hearts.[324] In chapter 27, Kótan places eight medallions, each containing one of the inscriptions on the eight towers, on the sacred necklace. Thus, Archie wore these inscriptions close to his heart.

Sloth: K'ram'vl, dubbed "Sloth" by the old bearded knight, is introduced in chapter 7, along with Glutton, Liar, and Whiner. He represents those who receive the word but have no root and so fall away. "The one who received the seed that fell on rocky places is the man who hears the word and at once receives it with joy. But since he has no root, he lasts only a short time. When trouble or persecution comes because of the word, he quickly falls away."[325]

Splasher: In classical mythology, the dolphin was always associated with the Greek gods. It was quickly adopted as a Christian symbol of salvation, transformation, and love.[326] Splasher was a gift to Archie from Lord Pwrádisa (see "Pwrádisa" above), and he therefore represents the fact that salvation is a free gift from God.

Thlū'taku: Thlū'taku, introduced in chapter 5, represents Satan. Although he is not the legitimate master of any noble house, he is appointed steward over the six fallen houses. During the war, he takes the Tower of Peace as his headquarters and thereby represents the false peace that Satan gives to the world.[327] His shield has a black field with three green sharks.

---

324 Jeremiah 31:33.
325 Matthew 13:20–21.
326 Jack Tresidder, *The Complete Dictionary of Symbols.* San Francisco, CA: Chronicle Books, 2004.
327 Jeremiah 6:14; 2 Corinthians 11:14.

T'lantim: The T'lantim are the people of K'truum-Shra. The name is derived from the name "Atlantis" and has a plural ending—"im"—found in Hebrew (think cherubim and seraphim).

T'lôt'aris: T'lôt'aris is a knight in service to Lord Pwrâdisa. He represents the Holy Spirit, and to make him somewhat mysterious, he is frequently referred to simply as "the old bearded knight" or "the old knight," especially when he is instructing Archie. He uses the Socratic method of instruction (asking questions to lead his student to find the answers himself and to learn how to think critically). His name is derived from Aristotle, through whom we know about Socrates. His shield is a blue field with a white flame. The flame is a scriptural symbol of the Holy Spirit, for it is a purifying force.[328] It is also a heraldic symbol of zealousness.[329] Fire appears throughout the Bible as representing the presence of God, beginning with the non-consuming burning bush seen by Moses.[330] The angel of the Lord appeared as a pillar of flame to guide the Israelites through the desert.[331] Tongues of flame appeared over the heads of the disciples at Pentecost.[332] But the symbol is most significant in the novel because it is intended to show how trials test and purify the "metal" of faith.[333] Each time that Archie is tested, T'lôt'aris guides him in his testing.

Wheel: Archie's shield is a blue field with a white, eight-spoked wheel. This represents Archie's "invention" of the wheel, but more importantly, it represents the eight towers and his journey through the Beatitudes. Indeed, the wheel itself suggests a journey, for purpose of a wheel is movement. The eight-spoked wheel was an early Christian symbol,[334] for it could be drawn by superimposing the capital Greek letters making up the word, "fish," ΙΧΘΥΣ ("ichthus"),[335] one on top of another. The Greek letters

---

328 Hans Biedermann, *Dictionary of Symbolism: Cultural Icons and the Meanings Behind Them*. Translated by James Hulbert. New York: Facts on File, 1992.

329 Jack Tresidder, *The Complete Dictionary of Symbols*. San Francisco, CA: Chronicle Books, 2004; Ottfried Neubecker, *A Guide to Heraldry*. New York: Barnes & Noble, 2007.

330 Exodus 3:2.

331 Exodus 13:21.

332 Acts 2:3.

333 First Peter 1:1–7.

334 http://www.plymouth-church.com/ichthus.html (August 3, 2010); http://symboldictionary. net/?p=2963 (August 3 2010); http://www.timelesswoodturnings.com/ichthus_page.html (August 3, 2010); http://en.wikipedia.org/wiki/Icthus (May 2, 2010).

335 The Greek letter sigma is most often written as "Σ," but was sometimes written as "C." Thus, the word "ichthys" would normally be written as "ΙΧΘΥΣ," but in connection with the eight-spoked wheel symbol could be written as "ΙΧΘΥC."

spelling that word—iota, chi, theta, upsilon, and sigma—are an acrostic for the phrase, "Jesus Christ, God's son, savior," "Ιησους ('Iasus') Χριστος ('Christos'), Θεου ('theos') Υυιος ('huios'), Σοτηρ ('soter')," for they are the first letters of the Greek words making up that phrase.

Whiner: W'mat'thop, dubbed "Whiner" by the old bearded knight, is introduced in chapter 7, along with Glutton, Liar, and Sloth. He represents those who receive the word but are consumed by the worries of this life. "The one who received the seed that fell among the thorns is the man who hears the word, but the worries of this life … choke it, making it unfruitful."[336]

336 Matthew 13:22.

About the Book

Truth in the Eight Towers is intended to be a companion volume for the novel, **Archibald Zwick and the Eight Towers**, by the same author. While the novel is a Christian allegory, **Truth in the Eight Towers** is not only a serious study of the scriptures on which the novel is based, but is also a study of the symbolism supporting the allegory in the novel. Thus, **Truth in the Eight Towers** is an excellent resource for youth pastors and others leading groups reading the novel. Both books are available online from a number of retailers. For more information, visit the author's website, www.RobertLesliePalmer.com.

About the Author

Robert Leslie Palmer received a Bachelor of Arts *magna cum laude* with departmental honors in political science from Tulane University in 1979 and a Juris Doctor from Georgetown University in 1982. Following law school, he served as a Captain for four years in the United States Army Judge Advocate General's Corps, serving first with the Eighth Army in Seoul, Korea, and later with the First Cavalry Division at Fort Hood, Texas. After leaving the military, Palmer entered private law practice in Birmingham, Alabama.

In his practice, Palmer became aware of a terrible injustice in Alabama law, so in 2005 he founded the Alabama Legal Reform Foundation, a nonprofit organization of which he remains the president. For his successful reform effort he was nationally recognized by the Public Justice Foundation of Washington, D.C., which awarded him its "Access to Justice Award" in 2008. He was also named a "Champion of Justice" by the Alabama Association for Justice for the same successful campaign.

He has always enjoyed writing and in addition to publishing many law review articles, he has frequently written and published poetry and newspaper commentaries. On December 31, 2009, he sold his interest in his law firm so that he could write full time.

Palmer is a past president of the Birmingham chapter of the Christian Legal Society and he is currently the chairman of the board of directors of the Downtown Jimmie Hale Mission, Inc., a Christian-based, nonprofit 501(c)(3) organization, which includes a homeless shelter for men, a shelter for women and children, recovery programs, learning centers, and thrift stores.

CPSIA information can be obtained at www.ICGtesting.com

264166BV00001B/88/P

9 781615 078431